AF470967

THE DISNEYLANDS THAT NEVER WERE

Shaun Finnie

First Published by www.lulu.com 2006

Copyright © Shaun Finnie 2006

Shaun Finnie asserts the moral right to
be identified as the author of this work.

10 9 8 7 6 5 4 3 2

All rights reserved. No part of this publication may be
reproduced, stored in a retrieval system, or transmitted, in any
form or by any means, electronic, mechanical, photocopying,
recording or otherwise, without the prior permission of the
author.

ISBN 978 1 84728 543 0

THE DISNEYLANDS THAT NEVER WERE

CONTENTS

Introduction

THE DISNEY THEME PARKS AND RESORTS ARE favourite holiday destinations on three continents, with people travelling to visit them from every corner of the earth. There are currently eleven major Disney parks worldwide and there will most certainly be more built in the future.

For fans of this particular kind of entertainment, no-one does it better than Disney. The rides, the shows, the hotels, and their associated amenities are some of the best in the world.

But if the attractions that the Walt Disney Company have actually produced are this good, just imagine what other delights the Disney designers might have dreamed up, what wild fantasies they've come up with that have never seen the light of day.

Just imagine...

Imagine no more. It's time to step inside The Disneylands That Never Were.

Chapter 1 – From the Drawing Board

DISNEYLAND WAS ONE MAN'S DREAM. HE WAS A middle-aged businessman dreaming of a place where his entire family could enjoy themselves. He dreamed of a playground where everything would fit together in a consistent theme.

That dream of course belonged to Walt Disney, and he called his vision Mickey Mouse Park.

Disney's success had come from a long and popular series of short cartoons. After years of building the company only to lose everything when he discovered he didn't own the rights to the characters he'd created, Walt hit upon an idea for a mouse. He called this new character Mortimer. At the prompting of his wife Lillian, Mortimer became Mickey and Mickey, the little scamp who sang and whistled in what was mostly still the silent movie era, became an overnight sensation.

Emboldened by the success of Mickey Mouse and all the other characters in his short films, Walt dared to think the unthinkable. He decided to make a film the likes of which Hollywood had never even dreamed of before. Disney created a full length animated movie. Despite being called "Disney's Folly" by the rest of movie land and almost bankrupting the company, the film was eventually completed in 1937 and it was an immediate massive hit. Snow White and the Seven Dwarfs brought fame, acceptance and financial security to the studio.

Walt famously liked to say of his accomplishments, "It all started with a mouse". But speaking specifically of Disneyland, he also claimed, "It all started out from a daddy with two daughters wondering where he could take them where he could have a little fun with them too".

Like many people Walt worked long hours, often not getting home until after his daughters were asleep. The only real time he had with them was on Sundays. Sunday was Daddy's Day. Walt would take his girls to the park, put them on the swings and roundabouts and watch them enjoying themselves. The trouble was that it always irked him that the equipment was too small for him to ride alongside his daughters. There was nothing that the three of them could enjoy together. He would sit on a bench eating peanuts with the other fathers, all watching their children have fun. While that was nice, it wasn't enough. The eternal kid in Walt wanted to join in with them. "I was always trying to think of a place to take my two small daughters on a Saturday or Sunday afternoon, a place where I could have fun too", he said.

Other film companies were hosting tours of varying sizes around their facilities, and while this might have appealed to Disney it was obvious that visiting a room full of animators painting cells in Los Angeles would be nowhere near as exciting for visitors as seeing real live film stars, or at the very least some actual movie sets. Nevertheless Walt was also beginning to receive letters from children asking if they could come to visit the place where Mickey Mouse lived. He remembered how he felt with nowhere to take his daughters and combined this problem with the request in those children's' letters.

On the 31st of August 1948 Walt circulated a memo around the staff in his studio detailing his ideas for what he called "Mickey Mouse Park". Walt had already been considering providing his employees and invited guests with a quiet, leafy park where they could rest a while during their breaks. Initially the plan started out as little more than a field for picnics and perhaps baseball, though even the very first formal design was to include a whimsical singing waterfall. But his vision broadened after he visited the Henry Ford Museum at Greenfield Village, Michigan, and was struck by its layout. It combined plenty of attractions with a sense of space and old-time charm. This opened up all kinds of possibilities to him, but unfortunately when Walt had an idea that took his fancy, he often got carried away with it. In his mind the park rapidly grew to include a railway and even a little village. At other times his dreams would feature an old Western style settlement adjacent to an Indian encampment.

As these ideas began to take shape, Walt said, "I want it to be very relaxing, cool and inviting". However his older brother Roy, the company's money man, refused to finance the deal thinking that Walt would soon tire of it. Roy claimed of Walt, "He is more interested, I think, in ideas that would be good in an amusement park than in running one himself".

In the early 1940s Walt had moved his animation studio to a twenty-five building complex at Burbank's Riverside Drive. While this site was being constructed he realised that it contained enough ground for him to finally build the little park that children were writing for, the place where Mickey and the others characters lived.

Despite misgivings from Lillian (who, Walt liked to say, would ask him, "Why do you want to build an amusement park? They're so dirty!"), her husband gave serious consideration to a Burbank Entertainment Centre, to be situated on Riverside Drive, south of the Disney film studio.

This particular park never came to pass, and the plot of land where it was supposed to go now hosts California's Ventura Highway. The idea of the visitor's centre however was far from over.

Artist Harper Goff was working at the Warner Brothers Studio when Walt hired him to help design the theme park. Goff's first concept drawing for the park in 1951 included an old mining town, a water mill, a paddle steamer, bandstand, and a small settlement of Indian teepees. Goff was one of the very first Disney Imagineers. This was a word created by the Disney Company and refers to the designers, engineers, artists, architects, technicians etc involved in taking a ride, attraction, hotel or other theme park concept from its first little spark of imagination to a completed physical work fit for public presentation. It is a combination of the words imagination and engineer and represents, as Walt himself put it, "the blending of creative imagination with technical know-how".

The people who work under this title are usually employed by Walt Disney Imagineering, a subsidiary of the Walt Disney Corporation. Walt had become increasingly frustrated at not always getting finance for his theme park ideas, so in December 1952 he created WED Enterprises, a completely separate company funded with his own money. Named after the initials of its founder, Walter Elias Disney, WED had complete freedom to develop the technology necessary to create the rides and attractions he had in his mind. Prior to WED this collection of artists and engineers was called Walt Disney Inc. but changed its name almost immediately. Since 1986 this division of the company has been known as Walt Disney Imagineering. Its manufacturing arm, incorporated in 1965, was known as MAPO. MAPO took its name from MAry POppins, a movie which had forced some serious technological advances in order to get the action just as required. The film was such a huge financial success that it allowed the formation of WED's own full-time manufacturing team.

But that was all to come much later. Back at the birth of Imagineering Walt and Goff were beginning to map out Mickey Mouse Park in earnest. One of their earliest designs shows two small linked villages. One settlement would have included a town hall, bandstand and old-style department stores, much the same as we know Disneyland's Main Street today. The adjoining smaller village would have been in an older, Western style, complete with pony and stagecoach rides.

The visitor's centre would also have featured a corridor with glass walls so that the public could indeed look over the shoulders of animators, inkers and painters as they went about their daily tasks. Walt had originally thought that this would be boring for the visitors, but as more and more attractions were added to the park, watching the animators at work became seen as an acceptable option for guests to extend their stay.

Mickey Mouse Park would have also featured statues of the Disney cartoon characters, models of Gepetto's workshop, Snow White's cottage and a dwarf sized playhouse. Walt had already built a replica of the dwarves' cottage in his own back garden as a playhouse for his daughters, Sharon and Diane, and knew that this was the kind of thing that visitors to his park would be expecting to see.

And right from the very earliest designs the area available to the public would have featured one of Walt's passions – steam trains. The park was to have featured a small scale railroad which would carry authentic replicas of famous trains from history such as George Stevenson's Rocket.

Walt Disney was a self-confessed lifelong stream train fanatic. Since his earliest days in Kansas City he had seen the railroad as providing the path to excitement and adventure, and he wanted to bring that feeling into any studio tour or theme park he might create. He would even go as far as building his own small railroad, named the Carolwood Pacific, in his own considerably sized back garden.

A 1953 design map of Mickey Mouse Park shows an island marked Mickey Mouse Club after the famous "Mickey Mouse Club" TV series of the day. The television show was an entertaining and educational series for children, and a theatre to be located on the island was intended to replicate that format. It was hoped that some broadcasts of the actual show could come from this location too.

A concept drawing of the park from the following year depicted a Ferris wheel based on The Old Mill, Disney's Oscar winning Silly Symphony short featuring life in and around a decaying windmill. This idea resurfaced some four decades later when a small version of The Old Mill was built to hold a sandwich and snacks kiosk in Disneyland Paris.

As Walt and his team of Imagineers came up with more and more ideas for his new venture, the name Mickey Mouse Park was starting to sound more and more restrictive. It had initially been dreamed up as simply a fictional home for his famous cartoon characters, but Walt soon had bigger ideas for the place he was now calling Disneylandia. This latest version of his dream project had now grown to include full sized models of buildings representing the values that made America great for Walt; values like hard work, family, and home. The first of these buildings would be the ramshackle rustic cabin that had featured in his 1949 movie "So Dear to My Heart". It was important to Walt that he combined education with the sense of fun that he hoped visitors would get from a visit to his park. "I don't just want to entertain kids with pony rides and swings", he said. "I want them to learn something about their heritage".

The park would also feature a small dancing figure in the little town's Opera House. Walt brought in famous song and dance man of the day Buddy Ebsen, who was filmed performing against a grid lined background so that the animators could track the dancer's moves more easily. They constructed a little figure based on the entertainer and, using a series of rods hidden beneath the small stage, the small model man could be made to perform a crude but passable imitation of Ebsen's dance routine. This basic audio-animatronic technology was also to be used for a barber shop scene where a mechanical quartet would be seen singing "Down by the Old Mill Stream" in close harmony. As well as installing these figures in his park, Walt also had the idea of creating a succession of these miniature scenes, placing them in railroad cars and touring them around the country.

By this time the Disneylandia concept had grown to include a petting farm, skull rock, a fairground complete with carousel, a wild bird sanctuary on an island in a lagoon, and a canal boat ride which would wind past model scenes from Disney Animation classics. Walt also dreamed of a space ship and a submarine ride, but was adamant that there would be "No roller coasters or other rides in the cheap thrill category". Disneylandia would also include an old fashioned circus in a candy-striped tent. And in a hand written note on another of Harper Goff's maps, in what looks very much like Walt's handwriting, is scrawled a single word ringed in red pencil.

"Castle".

The concept of a central castle was something that changed many times over the park's evolution. A design based upon Cinderella's castle from the animated Disney movie was considered, as was a wooden Robin Hood castle from the 1952 Richard Todd film. Some designs did away with the castle completely, while others had a completely different fantasy design.

As the scope of the park grew Walt knew that if he wanted to produce it as he imagined it, then he would need a lot of extra capital. All the banks that he approached refused to loan him the money, so he negotiated a partnership deal with the television company ABC. Disneylandia was the name that he went to ABC with to secure additional funding for the park's construction. His innovative idea of tying Disneylandia to a weekly series of the same name appealed to the TV people but they had one suggestion. They disliked the name, considering it confusing and too exotic. Walt accepted their money and also their suggestion for a new, simplified name; Disneyland.

Disneyland would be split into a series of smaller themed areas Lands, all arranged like spokes around a central hub. Some of the early ideas thrown around for these permanent Lands included the miniature buildings of Lilliputian Land, and True-Life Adventure Land, named after the award winning series of nature films that the company had made. True-Life Adventure Land might also have included a Pirate's Shack and Blackbeard's Den. Even this long ago the plans for these two highly detailed walkthroughs introduced the pirates' theme that would reappear so successfully at Disneyland in later years.

Lilliputian Land was an extension of the earlier canal boat concept which would later appear at most of Disney's sites, but this time the "giant" guests would float passed miniature versions of various landmarks from around the world.

While the Snow White and Peter Pan rides that can still be found in Disneyland today were already in place on the earliest maps, there were also illustrations of a couple of other planned walk-through Fantasyland-style attractions. Had they gone into production, these would have been based on the tales featuring Mother Goose and Alice in Wonderland.

Although his vision was now considerably larger than the original Mickey Mouse Park idea, Walt was still eager to have his cartoon stars represented in the new park. Donald Duck was hugely popular in the 1940s and '50s, so it would seem logical to feature him on some kind of boat ride. The boats suggested wouldn't have provided a gentle ride though. In keeping with the duck's playful spirit, Donald Duck's Bumper Boats were to have been small engine-powered, one- or two-seat craft capable of bumping into one another without real damage. They would have effectively been floating versions of the bumper cars seen in many fairgrounds.

Legendary Imagineer John Hench claimed that Walt wanted a small park filled with nice little details, like a singing waterfall, but eventually the number of things he wanted to include outgrew the space that was available to him at Burbank. It was time once again to look for a new site.

Walt's vision for Disneyland may have changed radically from his view of the original small Mickey Mouse Park, but he was still sure of one thing: the park would be like nothing else on earth. He said, "Disneyland is like Alice stepping through the looking glass. To step through the portals of Disneyland will be like entering another world".

And at the time even the great Walt Disney couldn't have known how right he was.

Chapter 2 – The Birth of Disneyland

IN LATE 1953 WALT FINALLY SETTLED ON A location for his land. There was a 160 acre orange grove at the junction of Harbor Boulevard and the Santa Ana Freeway which met his requirements perfectly. It was at a major highway intersection, allowing easy access for visitors from all around California and further afield, and best of all there was plenty of land available for purchase at a reasonable price. Or so Walt thought. This would prove to be the one thing that he regretted about the site in later years. When the construction and location of Disneyland was announced, the plots of land immediately around those owned by Disney were quickly snapped up by quick-thinking entrepreneurs. Today they are the sites of motels and fast food chains, something that Walt disliked intensely, as he felt their presence tarnished the approach to his playground. It also severely restricted any ambitions for future expansion, as it continues to do to this day.

After the Mickey Mouse Park and Disneylandia plans had more or less fully evolved into 'Disneyland', Walt and his brother Roy felt confident enough to take out front page adverts in Southern California's newspapers. Announcing the park under the headline, "Walt Disney Make-Believe Land Project Planned Here", The Burbank Review claimed that Disneyland would be "Something of a fair, an exhibition, a playground, a community center, a museum of living facts and a showcase of beauty and magic."

It was to be all of these things and more, but not immediately. After almost twenty years of planning, Walt finally opened the world's first theme park on 15th of July 1955. There were plenty of amusement parks before this time – and Walt visited many of them to establish precisely what he didn't want his own park to become – but this was the first one that had coherent themes running through it; Disneyland was the first true theme park in every sense. It had just eighteen rides and attractions to entertain the invited guests, and the opening day was nothing short of a disaster, but at least it opened on time.

Since then the ideas for upgrading the park have been many and varied, but initially there wasn't a whole lot more than curiosity to entice the crowds. They wouldn't come in the required numbers unless they could see exactly what they'd be getting for their entrance money. It was time to use a new form of advertising.

Walt had used money from a TV deal to finance the development of the park, and for his part of the bargain he was to provide ABC with a weekly TV show. But this was to be no normal presentation. Walt used the rapidly growing medium of television to promote interest in his Anaheim attraction. An article in TV Guide magazine discussed the series, but also focussed on the fact that the park would be opening pretty soon. It added, "By that time there will be hardly a living sole in the United States who won't have heard about the Disneyland Amusement Park and who won't be dying to come see it." This gushing prose had of course been written by one of Disney's own advertising staff.

But even the Disneyland that finally opened its gates was not the one that had been advertised. The first promotional materials had mentioned True-Life Adventureland, Lilliputian Land, The Rivers of Romance, The World of Tomorrow, and a Spaceship To The Moon. There would also have a large recreational park, a simple area of grassland for the kids to run around, and just outside the boundaries of the small park, a baseball diamond and a picnic area.

A new section named Frontierland was soon added. Davy Crockett was a huge fan favourite in the 1950's mainly due to Disney's television series featuring Fess Parker as the famous frontiersman. Disney intended to capitalise on this by creating a Frontierland Wax Museum. This concept didn't last long when the company began to successfully develop their audio-animatronics, but figures of Crockett and Daniel

Boone were constructed. For a while they were displayed at the park, but eventually, in an era of space flight and lifelike moving figures, the wax museum idea wasn't deemed 'special' enough.

The part of the park that had been announced as The World of Tomorrow was quickly renamed Tomorrowland. Much of this area of the park was designed by Imagineer John Hench. In fact Hench has been responsible for so much of the look of Disneyland over the years that Walt would occasionally tell people, "I'm not Walt Disney – he is", playfully pointing at his friend and colleague.

One of Hench's early Tomorrowland ideas was a fun study of animated numbers in an attraction named Mathmagicland. This took its name and overall idea from the classic short movie, Donald in Mathmagicland, an award winning movie which featured the famous duck learning all manner of numerical lessons. In the film Donald learned that mathematics is important in all our daily lives even if we don't realise it. Donald was given examples of the relevance of numbers using everything from stringed musical instruments to the use of angles in a game of pool, and visitors to this attraction would be taught in a similar way.

Another of John Hench's ideas for Tomorrowland that never made it past the planning stages was a variation of Astro-Jets, Orbitron, and Disney's other 'Dumbo in the air' rocket rides. This carousel-style spaceship ride would have been situated inside a dimly lit room and was to include light and sound effects that would later be used in Hench's plans for Space Mountain.

From opening day through to the twenty-first century, many visitors to the park are looking to see the famous Disney characters, so an attractive ride that also featured the characters in some way would be doubly appealing. For example Pinocchio, the puppet who longed to be a real live little boy, is the star of Pinocchio's Daring Journey. This dark ride which closely follows the plot of the film in a series of dioramas is a favourite with visitors to Fantasyland. However this was not the first Pinocchio ride planned for Disneyland. In the early plans for the park guests would ride in boats through the belly of Monstro the whale and past forlorn-looking models of the little wooden boy and his father, Geppetto the toymaker. This gentle ride would suddenly become a turbulent log flume as the boat fell sharply down the whale's gigantic tongue and out of his mouth. Upon leaving the ride guests would have found themselves in a little Italian piazza named Pinocchio Square.

According to one set of plans Fantasyland was also to have included a huge figure of a crocodile in the lagoon. This was an oversized version of Captain Hook's nemesis from Peter Pan. He would have had his head resting on the banking with his mouth gaping wide open. The rather disconcerting aspect of this attraction was that guests would be expected to walk straight into his open jaws. Once inside they would descend a few steps into the creature's dimly-lit stomach area. From here they would have an excellent view through large picture windows of the tropical fish that could be seen swimming in the lagoon itself. Unfortunately that was all that the planned attraction had to offer. Although its external appearance was novel, the fact remains that it was simply an unusual aquarium, and so it was left on the drawing board.

Another small section of the park was designed by Bill Justice, the creator of the loveable chipmunks Chip 'n' Dale, but never made it past his drawing board. Justice worked on Dumbo's Circus, to be situated near Storybook Land in Fantasyland. This was to have presented audio-animatronic versions of the humorous elephant pyramid and fire fighting clown sections of the classic movie about the little flying elephant. And of course Dumbo himself was to feature, flying high above the paying public.

It wasn't just Disney's cartoon characters that were planned to feature in Disneyland's first years though. The Disney studio also owned the rights to The Wizard of Oz and other L. Frank Baum books. They designed a small Land Of Oz section in the early days of the park to feature Dorothy, the Scarecrow, and the other famous Oz characters. The designs weren't viewed favourably at the time but later, when a Rock Candy Mountain ride was planned as an initial expansion of Storybook Land, some of the unused Oz plans were resurrected. It was thought that they might form the basis or a ride inside this confectionary peak but once again nothing came of it. Had it ever come to pass, Rock

Candy Mountain would have loomed large over the entrance to the Storybook Land / Lilliputian Land boat ride.

The tiny buildings that the Storybook Land Canal Boat Ride winds past today were actually meant to be small demonstration models. Walt had intended for all these buildings to eventually be built full scale. As both time and money were running out leading up to opening day, the tiny models were planted in the park as a temporary measure. When it became clear that the little buildings were drawing favourable responses and were going to stay in place, a visual gag was designed whereby a sleeping giant would be among the miniature houses. As he gently snored, his breath would turn the sails of a tiny windmill but sadly he's another great idea that we were destined never to see.

The Matterhorn bobsled ride was a personal favourite of Walt's. He'd wanted to recreate the peak from his movie The Third Man on the Mountain. But the finished version at Disneyland differed from Walt's original vision though. The attraction began life as plans for a simple toboggan ride running down Disneyland's Holiday Hill, the little mound of dirt that separated Fantasyland from Tomorrowland. Then once the Matterhorn came into the frame Walt envisioned actual, free running bobsled cars thundering through the mountain on a man-made ice run instead of speeding along a steel track as they do today. Thankfully his team of Imagineers were able to convince him that the inherent safety issues would make it unworkable, and the metal tubing system was implemented instead. It was still on the site of Holiday Hill though, but this little peak had changed its name by now to Snow Hill in preparation for the bigger mountain's construction.

Let's take a moment out here to define a term. A Disney 'dark ride' is usually a fairly slow moving attraction with visitors seated in some kind of car travelling along a track. The ride vehicle will typically enter a darkened show building and the track will wind past scenery and figures. All these will be decorated using special paint that glows brightly when lit by a special 'black light'. As they are they only things that show up under this light, anything decorated with the glowing paint shines brightly in the darkness, providing a kind of cinematic effect. It's a hugely effective lighting trick that has been widely used by Disney from the company's earliest attractions to the present day.

In the 1970's, a dark ride based upon the animated Robin Hood movie was considered, but it was quickly realised that there was little that could be done with it. While movies are at heart based upon strong storylines and characterisations, a theme park ride based on that same movie has to rely purely upon the visual aspect of the film. So while the Robin Hood movie may be fun, any ride based upon it would have had to be set in a forest, with very little to offer in the way of visual stimulation and inspiration for the Imagineers.

Tron, on the other hand was a film that had very strong and very distinctive visuals, being set for the large part inside a video game. Rides were designed based on both this movie and another sci-fi live action film, The Black Hole. However as neither movie was the box-office success that had been hoped, plans for both were abandoned.

Had Disney scored a big hit with The Black Cauldron, then this film too would have given birth to a ride of its own. Again, the film died and again the plans for an associated attraction died with it. The interesting thing about this proposed ride was that it would have had a switching track, allowing various routes to be created throughout the attraction. In this way the park visitor would have had an experience that changed each time they rode it.

One film-based attraction that did make it all the way to installation was Indiana Jones and the Temple of the Forbidden Eye This is a huge ride, involving guests riding in trucks and avoiding all sorts of perils in the style of an Indiana Jones adventure. And, thanks to the controlling computers, this journey does indeed change from one ride to the next. But even this was nowhere near the attraction that was originally planned. It was in the modelling stages when three of the four rides that would have been there were cut. Only the main headline ride remained within the Indiana Jones building.

There are always long lines to ride through the Temple of the Forbidden Eye, just as there always were to take the now-demolished Submarine Voyage, another favourite with many visitors to Disneyland. Time will tell if the replacement Finding Nemo ride will create its own generation of fans, but perhaps those who loved the old Submarine Voyage might not have been so enamoured by the underwater cruise had it been completed as originally designed. It was initially meant to be a simple Glass Bottom Boat ride, with guests crowded around a central viewing area before Walt settled on the idea of creating the world's largest privately owned fleet of submarines.

After this forty year old attraction closed there was talk of converting the lagoon into a journey through the undersea world of Ariel, the Little Mermaid. Like many other rides based on this tale, it wouldn't happen.

One of the most fondly remembered attractions over the years at Tomorrowland has been Adventure Thru Inner Space. The ride 'shrunk' guests as it carried them through first a snowflake, then a single water molecule and finally to the heart of an oxygen atom. But this famous ride had been adapted from earlier plans for a proposed Adventures in the Micro World attraction, also known as Trip Through a Drop of Water. While Adventure Thru Inner Space concentrated on the atomic structure of water, the earlier theme for the attraction was to have been more biology than physics. It would have had riders being shrunk to the size of protozoa in a dark ride depicting the sometimes frightening microscopic organisms found in an everyday drop of water.

A further Tomorrowland idea was Adventures in Science, a ride which would show guests the wonders of the galaxy and the formation of the planets. This was scheduled as an early expansion to Disneyland, on the site of what would eventually become Space Mountain. There was also to have been an interactive section to this attraction. Just like today's Innoventions, this would have been a showcase for technology and fun, where guests could have learned about science and how technology was improving their lives, both now and in the foreseeable future, in an entertaining way.

All of these attractions would have been welcome additions to Disneyland. But some of the park's other lost expansions were planned on a much larger scale.

Chapter 3 – Disneyland's Other Main Streets

AFTER SOME WELL DOCUMENTED INITIAL OPENING day problems Disneyland quickly began to draw huge crowds and Walt immediately started planning new additions to his park. There was much that he had wanted to include from the very beginning but funds would not allow. Now he had the chance to expand his playground and in doing so encourage repeat visits from guests eager to see what Disney would come up with next. As he said, "It's something that will never be finished, something that I can keep developing and adding to". A year after opening the park he announced that he would be doing just that, adding an entire new street to the park.

The first area that guests have always found themselves in as they enter Disneyland is Main Street USA. This quaint street is often said to resemble

Marceline, Missouri, where the young Walt Disney had spent some of his formative years. While it's true that Walt wanted to recreate the spirit of small-town America from that time, the actual look of the street is probably a combination of influences from Marceline and Fort Collins, Colorado. This was the hometown of Imagineer Harper Goff, who drew many of the early sketches for Main Street.

One of the first drawings of Disneyland had shown Main Street ending with a small residential area. This was soon replaced by the central hub and castle that we see today, but Walt kept the idea of having a residential area complimenting the commercial Main Street to one side. He reasoned that it was a good idea that might become useful at some later point.

The plot behind the eastern side of Main Street USA was initially just being used as a lumberyard and was a prime target for any expansion. Walt and his Imagineers returned to the theme of a residential area, and realised that this undeveloped piece of the park would be ideal for a second street running parallel to Main Street.

Market Street or, as it was called in later design revisions, Residential Street came so close to being constructed that it is clearly shown on one of Disney's promotional maps from 1956. The small dusty street full of quaint dwellings was at first going to run past a small town church and lead up to a dilapidated 'haunted house' sitting at the top of a hill. However, Walt didn't like the thought of a building looking so run-down in his beautiful park, so the idea of the spook house was killed off. But like all good ghosts, it would eventually return.

Walt Disney made no secret of the fact that he loved travelling. He was especially fascinated by Europe and adored the cluttered old cities that were so vastly different from the places he had grown up in. It was this idea of excitement waiting around every disorganised corner that he was trying to convey when he presented the idea of International Land. This proposed Disneyland expansion, which was eventually trimmed down to a smaller International Street, extended upon the idea of Market Street and was to have given guests a feeling of what those twisting and turning jumbled streets were like in towns and countries that they would perhaps never visit for themselves. Switzerland, Germany, Denmark, Japan, Spain and France were all suggested for being represented in this series of small lanes to be built at the outer edge of Tomorrowland. Guests would be able to take in all this foreign architecture, and all the small alleys would lead to an Italian village square, the central hub of International Street.

One of the big draws of International Street would have been a very special Chinese restaurant. Some plans indicate that instead of the multi-national street, there was to be an entire Chinatown district designed around this dining hall. As well as having a live singing group supported by audio animatronic singing birds, the restaurant would have featured a talking dragon built into the walls. This long-bodied lizard was to act as

Master of Ceremonies and introduce an animatronic wise-cracking Confucius figure, voiced by the Golden Horseshoe Review's legendary Pecos Bill himself, Wally Boag. Unlike later, more complex Disney park figures, the Chinese philosopher would have to remain seated for the entire performance with only his head moving. Even so, the Imagineers still couldn't get even this limited amount of movement to operate correctly. The human robotic Confucius simply wasn't of good enough quality to hold the show, but the singing animatronic birds worked fine. In fact they were so impressive that they became the first audio-animatronics to be displayed to the public.

One of the things that Walt had wanted to be included in the park was The Enchanted Tiki Room. No, this wasn't to be an early version of the long-running show "where the birds sing words and the flowers croon", but a Hawaiian themed restaurant with the same name. After Disneyland's Chinese restaurant plans were abandoned, John Hench designed this restaurant to provide diners with South-Seas styled entertainment while they sampled an authentic Polynesian meal. Guests would be serenaded by the singing Tiki Gods, flowers and parrots while they were served a three course meal. The singing theatre was created pretty much as Hench had planned, but the dining-room portion was removed. The problem was obviously that the show element was of a fixed time length, but people like to eat their food at different speeds.

All of this International Street proposition would have been situated between Tomorrowland and Main Street and was supposed to have opened just a year after the rest of the Disneyland. A board was displayed in the park's Hub between Main Street and Tomorrowland stating that International Street would be opening here in 1956. Then the date on the sign changed to announce that the new street was coming in 1957, then '58, but no construction work ever seemed to begin. The board was eventually quietly removed.

This wasn't actually the end for International Street though. Even as late as the 1980s the Imagineers were coming up with ideas to bring a series of new attractions to Disneyland, all of them linked by their representation of a different geographical location. International Street would have covered this, but by now it had been relocated to the area behind the Haunted Mansion. An early version of the Maelstrom ride from Epcot's interpretation of Norway would have been seen here, and there were also plans for an Alpine skiing simulator as well as attractions based in Paris and medieval England.

While plans for International Street were ultimately abandoned (though its basic theme of foreign shops and restaurants would of course resurface in the design of Epcot), the idea of having a second street run parallel to Main Street was still an attractive one. The version of this that has probably come closest to being built at Disneyland was called Liberty Street. This was to have represented the original thirteen American colonies of the 18th century and would have featured static wax tableaux of Presidents and inventors in a show called One Nation Under God. It would have also included displays featuring the signing of the Declaration of Independence, the Statue of Liberty and the Liberty Bell. There would have been a small fleet of ships in Griffin's Wharf, Liberty Street's small harbour, and away at the end of the street there would have once again been a haunted house. Sound familiar? Much of the concept survived to become Liberty Square, which eventually opened at Walt Disney World on the other side of the country some fifteen years later. The inventors were removed from One Nation Under God and the attraction renamed The Hall of Presidents, but early versions of this were still only to comprise of static waxworks.

Plans for Market, Residential, International and Liberty Streets were all scrapped, but their ideas gave birth to many attractions around Disney's world in the future. And the concept of another lane or two running parallel to Main Street finally came to life, after a fashion, decades later at Disneyland Paris. The site features covered arcades stretching behind the stores on both sides of Main Street which are, incidentally, a great way of avoiding the crowds. In one of these arcades is a tableau of the building and delivery of the Statue of Liberty, just as was planned for Disneyland back in the 1950's. As we'll see repeatedly in these pages, Disney never fully rejects an idea. They just store them away for possible later use.

Edison Square

Some plans for Disneyland's expansion had the second street parallel to Main Street ending in a small, enclosed area that would have been named Edison Square. Set in New York or Chicago of 1910, this was another suggested expansion that would, like the proposed Market Street, have emphasised the residential aspect of the area as a counterpoint to the commercial theming represented by Main Street.

"Main Street, U.S.A. is America at the turn of the century, the crossroads of an era", said Walt. "The gas lamps and the electric lamp, the horse-drawn car and the auto-car." Had it ever been built, Edison Square would have depicted the birthplace of those social leaps forward.

Walt had always been fascinated with inventors and inventions, especially his boyhood hero Thomas Edison. He loved the idea of a portion of his park honouring technological progress in day-to-day life. Edison Square would have been both thematically and physically situated between Main Street USA and Tomorrowland. It would show the advances in household appliances from the time of Walt's boyhood up to the present day and beyond, providing a link between the Main Street's turn-of-the-century past with the idealised future of Tomorrowland.

Had it gone ahead, Edison Square would have probably opened in 1959 as an expansion after Liberty

Street (or one of the other Residential Street concepts) had been established for a year or two. Its proposed headline attraction was to be Harnessing The Lightning, a cul-de-sac made up of four walk-through theatres hidden behind facades of urban town houses. As guests were ushered from theatre to theatre they would first see an American home as it would have been in the gaslight days before electricity. Audio animatronic figures were designed to show how life was in those days. The next scene would present the same home just as it received electric lighting, before the audience moved on to a third theatre showing the house with the time-saving electrical appliances of 'today'. In the final set, guests would see the robot actors explaining how tomorrow's technological advances might be brought into their daily lives in a possible future Electric Age.

Unfortunately, as with the Confucius dinner theatre planned for International Street, the audio animatronics that Harnessing The Lightning would have required were simply not sophisticated enough in the mid-1950's to make the attraction work, and it was reluctantly shelved. With its signature attraction gone, there was no justification for the building of Edison Square and it was quietly forgotten. The great inventor Thomas Edison never got his own Land at Disneyland, but he has received many tributes around the Disney parks in the form of plaques, portraits, and commemorative windows.

The old lumber yard that Edison Square and its residential street would have occupied is now used for storing parade floats. It also contains The Inn-Between, a pleasant pre- or post-shift restaurant for cast members. This same area would later be considered as the site of Hollywoodland, a new Land that would also be touted for Florida's Disney – MGM Studios park as part of The Disney Decade.

And the Harnessing The Lightning idea? Less than a decade later the concept was resurrected and, with the addition of a revolving theatre, proved a huge success at the 1964 / 65 World's Fair.

Chapter 4 - All The World's A Fair

PERHAPS THE 1964 / 65 WORLD'S FAIR DOESN'T strictly belong in this book as, unlike most of the other things described, the Fair and Disney's contributions to it actually were presented to the public. But it's worth looking a little at the history of this event and its influence on Walt Disney's future theme park plans.

Walt wanted to expand his Californian theme park. His idea was always for Disneyland to be ever-changing, and he had grand ideas for additions to it. But nothing was going to be installed that wasn't perfect, or at least working correctly. Building Disneyland had consumed all the cash and goodwill that Walt and his brother Roy had been able to beg or borrow. They needed some way to test out ideas for new attractions and ride mechanisms, but hopefully they could get someone else to pay at least part of the development costs.

And that's when fate stepped in.

By the late 1950's Disneyland had become firmly established as a major Californian crowd-puller, but ever the perfectionist, Walt was disappointed that it was only regularly attracting visitors from around a quarter of the USA. He figured that the rest of the country would be as receptive to the Disneyland concept as the west coasters had been. Although he has often been quoted as saying that there would never be another Disneyland, he was starting to get offers of help from investors and States to set up similar parks in other parts of the country. While publicly he was concentrating on planning additions and improvements to his current park, privately Walt had already commissioned a feasibility study that showed overwhelming favour for an east coast version of Disneyland. There were however doubts that the supposedly more sophisticated eastern populous would accept the simple delights that Disney was offering. Then in 1960 Walt heard that New York was to host the 1964 / 65 World's Fair to coincide with that city's 300th anniversary.

The World's Fair had been operating since its inception in London in 1851, presenting expositions every few years in various cities around the globe. Walt loved them and all that they represented as they showed the best that the world had to offer, both now and potentially in the future. He had even donated a Mickey Mouse cartoon to the Nabisco pavilion at the 1939 Fair in New York City. Also he had been brought up on tales of these events as his father, Elias Disney, had been a carpenter at the World's Fair in Chicago, seventy years previously

Walt realised that if he managed to get involved in the New York City Fair then he could reap multiple benefits. It would be possible to allay fears of east coast reluctance to his particular brand of entertainment, create attractions that would be ready-made for installation at Disneyland when the Fair finished, receive free advertising, and finally raise much needed research and development revenue. This last point was especially important as the lack of advancement in robotics technology was holding up major developments that were needed to get people coming back to the park for return visits.

The World's Fair just might provide the answer. Walt knew that much of corporate America would feel that it had to be represented at such a large and prestigious New York event but that the businessmen wouldn't have a clue about what form of entertainment they should provide. He could help them, and in return they would be helping him to create Disneyland attractions that would live on long after the Fair had closed. But Walt figured that there was no way that any attraction of this size could make money in two years, it would take much longer than that to recoup its development costs. So rather than supply their own attractions, the Disney company contacted many of the top corporations in the States, offering to create attractions at the Fair for them. Time was tight though;

there was less than four years to develop anything, as the Fair was to open on April 22nd, 1964.

One of the companies that Walt spoke with was General Motors, who were very enthusiastic about the Fair. So much so in fact that they designed their own huge pavilion named Futurama, a design for future life on the earth, under the seas and out in space, without requiring Disney's assistance. The G.M. people did however suggest that Walt talk to Ford. He did just that, and found Ford very receptive to his suggestions. The Disney-built Ford Wonder Rotunda was huge (more than twice the size of today's Pirates of the Caribbean ride) and contained many car-themed murals, indoor gardens and even the Auto Parts Philharmonic - an orchestra comprised entirely of automobile parts.

But the obvious highlight of the Ford Rotunda was a ride that had guests seated in the latest model Ford convertibles. They didn't even need to drive; the car itself took them on a 12-minute, 8-mph journey around the massive structure on a moving road called the Magic Skyway. First they toured the outside of the building from within giant Perspex tunnels which allowed views of almost the entire Fair show grounds. Then the Skyway tracks took the cars inside, through a swirling 'time tunnel' which strobed with rainbow lights, back to prehistoric times, where audio animatronic cavemen were seen discovering fire and inventing the wheel. Further along were the famous battling dinosaurs that would end up in the Primeval World diorama on the Disneyland Railroad. Eventually the vehicles deposited guests at Space City, where they could see the technology of the immediate future. Spaceship Earth would later resurrect many of these ideas at Epcot.

Ford provided one hundred and sixty actual production cars to be installed in the ride. Each was then completely gutted and had a special "radio" fitted which could play the ride commentary in one of six selectable languages. However major problems arose with the timing of the free rolling cars on the Disney-designed track. Because the different models of car were of varying weights and sizes – and so were their passengers - they travelled along the moving track at different speeds, leading to some inevitable collisions. In the Fair's early days the problem was so bad that they had a repair shop built into the attraction.

While visiting a Ford plant, Walt and Imagineer John Hench saw a kind of conveyor belt being used to transport hot metal ingots. The pair soon worked out that this idea could be adapted for moving people on rides, eliminating the need for wheeled carriages. Disney first used the resulting Peoplemover track system on the Magic Skyway, and has since used it to transport guests on many of its theme park rides like Haunted Mansion, Spaceship Earth, Horizons and others.

The plans for the Harnessing the Lightning walk-through attraction from the abandoned Edison Square were revived, adapted and offered to General Electric under the new name of The Carousel of Progress. John Hench and Walt came up with the idea of combining the scenes of the attraction within a revolving theatre in order to fit the maximum number of visitors and the biggest show possible into the relatively small area that General Electric had been allocated at the Fairground.

While it is the best remembered attraction from the Progressland pavilion, the Carousel of Progress wasn't the only attraction that Disney created for General Electric. The Progressland show building was a huge flattened three-storey illuminated dome that contained five separate shows. A huge 'Kaleidophonic' display that pulsed with coloured starbursts in time to music and narration led to the Carousel of Progress entrance. The Carousel itself was much like we see it today at Walt Disney World's Magic Kingdom, with the four stages of electrical development introduced by the father and his dog.

This show probably has more of Walt's own ideas and personality in it than any other Disney attraction ever built. It's filled with nostalgia for his Midwestern youth. He personally picked the voice actors, wrote large portions of the script, and showed the animatronics programmers how the characters should move. Even the idea of having a dog in each scene was Walt's idea, using it as a humorous link while the father emphasised the sponsor's message of household progress through electrical appliances. And General Electric was more than happy with the number of people that were hearing that message. The Carousel of Progress could be shown to almost four thousand potential G.E. customers per hour, with each section of the theatre holding two hundred and fifty people.

When it was presented at the World's Fair, guests leaving the Carousel of Progress would have been able to enter Medallion City, an all-electric home of the future. But by the time the attraction was relocated to Disneyland, the post show area had changed.

After exiting the Disneyland version of the Carousel's final theatre, guests boarded an escalator to the top level of the building which housed a 160-foot scale model of Progress City, the city of the future. Originally the ride was to have continued up here and guests would have been able to view the model whilst still seated in their vehicles. This model would later become part of Walt's original plan for Epcot, and a large portion of it can still be seen at Walt Disney World, from the Tomorrowland Transit Authority as it passes through Space Mountain.

Heading back down to the lowest level of Progressland, World's Fair visitors could watch an actual demonstration of controlled thermonuclear fusion. This might seem alarming to us today, but in the 1960s nuclear power was seen as cheap, clean and safe. Thankfully, the U.S. Atomic Energy Commission had declined the Fair's organisers' request that they also take a real mobile nuclear fission plant to the show grounds.

The Fair had an adult entrance cost of $2, with many of the pavilions charging an additional entrance fee. However, General Electric's Progressland pavilion was free. This fact, combined with the novelty of the Carousel of Progress show, ensured that Progressland became one of the most popular exhibits at the Fair.

Walt had asked both Ford and General Electric for $1million each for the use of his name on the attractions that his company built for them at the Fair. When both readily agreed, Walt offered to offset this amount against shipping costs if he could install the attractions at Disneyland. Both companies were invited to sponsor their attractions in California. While G.E. accepted, and The Carousel of Progress has gone on to delight generations of theme park visitors since it opened at Disneyland in 1967, Ford decided against it. The Magic Skyway was never seen again.

While Disney's exhibits for Ford and G.E. were corporate deals, Great Moments With Mr Lincoln would find its funding from a public source. The President of the New York World's Fair, Robert Moses, visited Walt in 1963 and was shown the designs and prototypes for an attraction called One Nation Under God. This had been planned for the abandoned Liberty Street area of Disneyland and was to have told the story of America's early political history culminating in an audio-animatronic show, which the Imagineers were calling The Hall of Presidents. Marc Davis and his team had got as far as producing a rough working model of Abraham Lincoln, who was to have been the centre-point of the show. This life-sized figure was shown to Moses, who was so impressed that he declared that he wouldn't open the World's Fair without the Lincoln model being there in one form or another. He immediately set about finding a sponsor to allow Disney the funds to speed up development.

Moses first approached the United States Federal Government with an ambitious plan for the full Hall of Presidents show, now re-titled We The People. When he met refusal in Washington, he took a cut-down version of the attraction to the State of Illinois, and offered them the chance to provide financial backing for this animated portrayal of their most celebrated son. They tentatively agreed, but it took a visit from Chicago-born Walt to his home state to calm fears that the show was going to trivialise the great statesman.

For years Walt had wanted to create a realistic life-sized human figure, seeing it as an extension of his two-dimensional animation. He had filmed an early test reel with actor and dancer Buddy Ebsen, translating his movements to a simple nine inch tall mechanical dancing man figure. Walt personally built much of the little scale vaudeville stage and mechanics to give life to the figure, which can now be seen in One Man's Dream at MGM Studios. Although the Dancing Man could perform along to a synchronised music track, he wasn't really sophisticated or reliable enough to perform before the public. Nevertheless, he holds a place in history as the first audio-animatronic human replica, and proved that this was possible.

A small Barbershop Quartet had also been built as an experiment in movement and sound co-ordination. But the construction of Mr Lincoln was a much more elaborate task and was, to put it bluntly, a rush job. He only passed his performance test at the Disney studios one week before the opening of the Fair, and was flown across the country the very next day. Unfortunately on arrival he was beset with problems. He got stuck in traffic that had built up for the opening of New York's new Shea Stadium, causing another day's delay before he could be assembled at the showground. And that's where the electrical problems started…

The damp New York air affected his wiring in a way that hadn't been foreseen in the drier climate of California, causing minor power losses which in turn gave the figure spasmodic, jerky movements. And when a creation as powerful as Mr Lincoln starts malfunctioning, it can cause serious damage. On one occasion when he went to sit on his chair, he seated himself successfully but then simply carried on lowering himself further down, shattering the wooden chair completely as he pushed himself to the ground. Other times he would wildly flail his limbs around, causing everyone to scurry for the power supply. Nobody wanted to receive a blow launched by five hundred pounds of hydraulic pressure.

Marc Davis wryly commented on the constant problems, "Do you suppose that God is mad at Walt for creating man in his own image?"

On 20th April 1964, just two days before the Fair was scheduled to open, Walt was to give a preview of the show to 500 assembled press and dignitaries. Unfortunately the Lincoln figure wasn't co-operating and Walt took the difficult decision to cancel the entire presentation, telling the expectant crowd, "There isn't going to be any show. It's not ready, and I won't show it to you until it is".

The animatronic President's malfunctions continued, and the World's Fair was forced to open without its anticipated Abraham Lincoln exhibit. Then suddenly a week later he began to work perfectly. Some have suggested that Walt held him back deliberately to increase media and public interest, and to make Lincoln appear to be the star of the show by arriving fashionably late. Whether this is true or not, there was huge media and public attention when the State of Illinois pavilion's Great Moments With Mr Lincoln finally opened on the 2nd of May 1964, and there was nothing else new to detract from it. The show was genuinely awe-inspiring, and huge crowds gathered to see the magnetic tape-driven 16th President read excerpts from his letters and speeches. When Mr Lincoln was first introduced he was seated and appeared to be a standard waxwork. But there were gasps of amazement when he stood up, cleared his throat and began to speak.

Back in the mid 1940's Walt had taken his wife Lillian on a holiday to New Orleans and in an antiques store there he discovered a small clockwork bird in a gilded cage. It was a French antique around 100 years old and Walt was fascinated by it. He took the little bird back to California with him where he had his engineers examine the mechanism to see how it worked. Walt figured that if engineers of a century ago could make a bird in a cage move and sing convincingly, then he and his team could perhaps work the same magic with a human figure.

The discovery of this little clockwork bird that sang, fluttered its wings and moved around on its perch was in Walt's eyes the birth of the audio-animatronic process that culminated with the production Mr Lincoln.

When the Enchanted Tiki Room had opened at Disneyland in 1963 its birds and flowers were the limit of audio animatronics at the time, with mechanisms not too far advanced from that tiny French cage bird. But the figures created for Flushing Meadow just a few months later were a massive leap forwards in robotic technology, with Abraham Lincoln being by far the most elaborate. Even his features were realistic, as Disney had managed to get hold of an actual death mask cast from the great man's face.

In the winter of 1964 that first figure was replaced with a more reliable version and on 18 July 1965 Great Moments With Mr Lincoln opened at Disneyland's Opera House. This is noteworthy in that it was the first time that any Disney attraction had appeared in two locations at the same time.

So Disney had provided the World's Fair with the Magic Skyway, Progressland and Great Moments With Mr Lincoln. But there was one late request to build another attraction, and this too would become an all-time Disney classic.

Walt had committed to supplying Ford, General Electric and the State of Illinois with shows for the Fair.

His people had been working on these projects for up to three years and were in a race against time to prepare them for the April 1964 opening date. Then in mid-1963 Pepsi-Cola decided that they needed an attraction for their pavilion to benefit the United Nations International Children's Emergency Fund – UNICEF. They arranged a meeting with a senior Disney executive, but with less than a year to go before the opening of the Fair they were told that the Imagineers were already over-stretched and that they wouldn't be able to take on another large endeavour such as this. When Walt heard of this he angrily, and perhaps predictably, rose to the challenge, saying, "I'm the one who makes those decisions. Tell Pepsi I'll do it!"

At short notice his Imagineers came up with a ride that has simultaneously become one of the most loved and annoying attractions in Disney's history, It's a Small World. This charming boat ride through the countries of the world perfectly illustrated the World's Fair's original theme of "Peace Through Understanding".

Artist Mary Blair set about creating the backgrounds and overall artistic design of the attraction, while Marc Davis was assigned to providing the actual nine minute ride and the characters. The building that housed It's A Small World was relatively plain compared to some of the architectural masterpieces that had been designed around the Fair, nothing at all like the elaborate façade of the Small World rides around the world today. Walt wanted something to help it stand out.

Rolly Crump was commissioned to design the Tower of the Four Winds, a beautiful 120 foot high, 200,000 pound collection of mobiles and pinwheels that stood at the entrance to the UNICEF pavilion. It could be seen from almost anywhere on the show ground and with over 100 moving parts it remains one of the most enduring memories of the entire Fair.

At first the ride was going to feature each country's national anthem as the boat floated past their scene, but it soon became clear that the different melodies would bleed into each other, becoming just a muddled noise. The ride needed a theme tune, one that was instantly memorable yet simple enough for young children to sing along with. The task of writing it went to the men who had recently provided the theme song for the Carousel of Progress, Richard and Robert Sherman. They wrote a simple round that could be sung in different languages. The first time Walt ever heard the song was when the brothers sang it unaccompanied, clapping out the beat, as they walked with him through a basic mock-up of the ride. The song has gone on to delight - and stick in the minds of - guests around the world for over forty years. After its success at the Fair, It's a Small World was transferred to Anaheim and opened at Disneyland in California in May 1966.

Both Small World and the Ford's Magic Skyway had guests board the ride vehicles outside the building. This was a technique that had already been used successfully at Disneyland. Park guests liked this approach because they could see that the ride was operational and how far the line stretched.

After seeing how successful the boat ride system proved on Small World, Walt suggested amending the Pirates of the Caribbean ride that was in the process of being built at Disneyland. The original walkthrough design was scrapped and a version of the Small World boat mechanism installed. At this stage however the figures in the Pirates attraction were still being thought of as static waxworks.

As the Fair's opening date drew closer, all development at Disneyland was put on hold, including preliminary work on what would eventually become the Haunted Mansion and Pirates of the Caribbean attractions. Everyone available was reassigned to World's Fair work, to the extent that when it came time to install the four attractions in New York, two hundred Disney employees were flown out east to assist.

The Fair ran for two seasons in 1964 and 1965 (it closed throughout New York's harsh winter period). It had two themes - "Peace Through Understanding" and "A Millennium of Progress" - and all contributors were asked to represent at least one of them. With nearly two hundred pavilions, this was the largest Fair to date. It covered almost six hundred and fifty acres; that's over twice the size of Walt Disney World's Epcot. The Epcot that we know today is in many ways a permanent World's Fair, showing examples of other countries and their cultures as well as the latest technological advances, and some areas that are educational as well as others that are just plain entertaining. All of this is brought together in one place yet grouped into many smaller pavilions. It's not too difficult to see the comparisons.

Quite a few African and Asian nations were represented by pavilions at Flushing Meadow, but hardly any European countries chose to attend, which lead to several individual U.S. states being invited. Many religious groups hosted pavilions too, further emphasising the "Peace Through Understanding" ideal.

As for the Progress motif, NASA displayed a huge rocket garden much like the one currently at Kennedy Space Centre in Florida, and many top American corporations, like IBM and Clairol, hosted pavilions. But there were also bars and dance clubs at the show ground which were late additions in an attempt to boost flagging attendance figures at the end of the first season. This and the non-appearance of many developed countries lead to the Fair being criticised for conservatism and commercialism, a far cry from its lofty aims of education and exploration.

Sadly Walt was eventually proved right; the Fair was a financial flop. However it was hugely successful for him and his company in a development and advertising sense. Over ninety percent of the Fair's visitors saw at least one of Disney's exhibits.

At its conclusion the Fair's president, Robert Moses, offered the land to Walt for an East Coast Disneyland. Walt politely declined. While it had been proven that people would come to Disney attractions on the Atlantic side of the country, he was concerned about the chilly climate so far north. If Disney were to ever build a park east of the Mississippi, Walt had a few much warmer sites in mind.

Chapter 5 – The Happiest Plans on Earth

DISNEY'S INVOLVEMENT WITH THE WORLD'S FAIR had provided the company with the impetus it needed for future growth at Disneyland. And the technological advances that the Fair's sponsors had required allowed for the commencement of two of the park's most enduring attractions.

As part of Disneyland's planned mid-sixties wave of expansion, Frontierland was to be augmented by a large covered shopping and dining area. The seedier aspects of frontier life would be depicted at the Thieves Market, a series of small alleyways winding between high buildings, where excitement and danger might be waiting around any corner. The general idea was sound, but the theming wasn't deemed specific enough. The focus of the Thieves Market shifted from a generic frontier area to the town of New Orleans and its name changed to the Blue Bayou Mart

Representing the twilight side of the Big Easy, the Blue Bayou Mart was to be permanently bathed in the same half-light that illuminates Disneyland's Blue Bayou restaurant today. While guests wandered through its narrow streets they might get caught in a sudden, unexpected rainstorm, or narrowly avoid the pull of quicksand.

With the addition of the Haunted House and the Pirates' Wax Museum this concept would evolve into the proposed New Orleans Square area of Disneyland. While the Thieves Market featured in the designers plans long enough to appear on several park maps, this section of the park went through quite a few changes before it finally opened to the public. And the same can certainly be said for the attraction that would have been situated in its basement.

Rogue's Gallery

Imagine a group of tourists following a Disneyland guide down dark, dank steps into what can only be described as a filthy dungeon. Imagine that dungeon being filled with static wax models and basic but effective audio-animatronic versions of some of the biggest villains and scoundrels ever seen on land or sea. A suitably dressed Disneyland guide might regale their tour group with a series of carefully scripted tales outlining the evil acts that these awful men and women had perpetrated, but making sure that the mood was lightened by adding a little grisly humour into the stories too.

Sound fun? How about if the tour group wasn't walking, but drifting along in boats, and the stories weren't simply told, but acted out in front of their eyes by lifelike moving robot figures?

This was the evolution of the Rogue's Gallery into the Pirates of the Caribbean.

Once Disneyland was financially secure, Walt began to think of ways to expand it. He knew that it needed bigger and better attractions than the impressive but small collection of rides and shows that were in place on opening day. One of his favourite ideas was to build a little piece of New Orleans right in the middle of California. The strangeness of it was attractively different from anything that the park held at the time. And the general eeriness of this planned New Orleans Square would be increased by the knowledge of what was in the basement - a series of waxwork tableaux featuring famous villains from history in a Rogue's Gallery.

The choice of these rogues was quickly narrowed down to just a collection of infamous pirates, and the suggested name of the attraction amended accordingly to The Pirates Wax Museum. In these revised blueprints, guests would still be walking through various scenarios like a tavern, or across the deck of a galleon, but now some of these tableaux would be introduced by animated characters, much like the then-groundbreaking father who could be seen and heard presenting the Carousel of Progress.

After the successful appearance of this figure and the incredible Mr Lincoln at the World's Fair, it seemed that Disney's robotic actors would be capable of almost anything. But there was real concern that crowds would form around the animatronics in the Rogue's Gallery instead of seeing them perform their spiel and moving on. With this in mind the attraction was changed once again. No longer would it be a simple walk through, now it was to become a guided tour. But this wouldn't solve the potential problem of long lines waiting their turn if the attraction were to prove as popular as was hoped.

The solution was staring them in the face. There were already pirate ships in the attraction, why not add some more smaller ones for the paying public? A boat ride with its predictable throughput patterns would be better than a walking tour that would only be able to proceed as quickly as its slowest group member. Once again, this was an idea that had been confirmed at the World's Fair, where the immensely popular It's a Small World ride had handled crowds in this manner.

Disneyland would eventually be invaded by pirates. But they wouldn't be the scariest new attraction to open in the park.

The Haunted Mansion

After the original decrepit ghost house that had been planned for Liberty Street had been rejected (Walt didn't want his vision of a beautiful, spotless Kingdom "spoiled" by a dusty, ramshackle building), the Imagineers tried many different ways to work the idea of a haunted house back into Disneyland. Various sketches were made, but none of these many early ghostly designs made it past Walt's critical eye. While the public might never have learned of these original plans to bring a few frights into the playground, Walt himself never forgot them.

On one vacation trip to England he was asked by the local press what the reason for his visit was. With a twinkle in his eye he told them that he had come to search country houses and old castles for ghosts that might be looking for a new site to haunt. He went on to claim that some souls of the dear departed might have been forcibly evicted from their ancestral homes during the heavy wartime bombing of the London Blitz. He jokingly suggested that Disneyland could create a retirement home for these and other homeless spirits.

These may have been throw-away lines to Walt, but they gave Imagineer Marty Sklar the idea for his famous 1963 invitation to the spirit world. Sklar designed a sign that hung outside what would become the Haunted Mansion in Disneyland. It read:

Notice!
All Ghost and Restless Spirits.

Post–lifetime leases are now available in this HAUNTED MANSION. Don't be left out in the sunshine. Enjoy active retirement in this country club atmosphere, the fashionable address for famous ghosts, ghost trying to make a name for themselves… and ghosts afraid to live by themselves! Leases include licence to scare the daylights out of guests visiting the portrait gallery, museum of the supernatural, graveyard and other happy haunting grounds

The earliest recorded story line for an actual haunted house tour was by Disney artist Ken Anderson in 1957. In this version a butler would lead a walking group of guests through the mansion house of Captain Gore, a distinguished old sea captain. As the butler lead the group through the creepy old house they would encounter secret passageways, moving portraits, arms reaching out to them from the walls and other pretty standard spooky house effects. However other actors would be seen gradually revealing the story of the sea captain's young bride who was murdered when she accidentally discovered that the respectable Captain Gore was in truth the notorious pirate Black Bart. The tour would finish with the dead bride's spirit revealing how she had tormented the dastardly captain until he couldn't take it any more, and his body was eventually found hanging in the attic.

A later, more light-hearted version of the walk-through had the spirit of Walt Disney himself leading guests through the house, or at least his tape recorded voice. Again, this reworking of the story fell apart due to the fact that all tour parties on foot travel at wildly varying speeds. Any presentation of this kind would rely on the Imagineers being able to predict the travelling speed and location of the viewer.

By 1959 two more Imagineers, Rolly Crump and Yale Gracey, had been brought on board to produce some of the wilder effects for the mansion. This was the same Mr Gracey whose name would eventually be used for the mansion's deceased owner. In one of Crump and Gracey's treatments of the story the sea captain and his proposed bride were to be married in Washington Irving's fictional town of Sleepy Hollow. The dreaded Headless Horseman would have been an unwanted wedding guest. This version of the show would have culminated with the ghosts of the less-than happy couple dissolving into waves of sea water which would flood the chamber. Just as the touring party were about to be soaked the tide would disperse as if it was never there. The dissolving of the ghostly figures and subsequent dispersal of the floodwater was created and tested with dramatic results. All Disney personnel who saw it remember it as one of the most amazing effects ever produced.

As Walt and the Imagineers couldn't decide on a storyline and coherent direction for the attraction, plans for the ghost house were temporarily shelved. Work pressed on with Disneyland's other major addition, Pirates of the Caribbean. Many of the lessons about crowd control that the Imagineers had been forced to learn for Pirates were easily implemented in The Haunted Mansion by the time it finally opened. Both attractions were converted from simple walk-throughs into complex rides.

Construction work on New Orleans Square began in 1961 and the building of the Haunted Mansion began a year later. An announcement was made that the Mansion would open in 1963 but by the time that year came around there was still no firm decision as to what shape the interior would take, so while the outside of the building was completed it was just an empty shell. Not only was the format of the attraction still undecided, but all the company's Imagineering resource had been moved to creating the attractions for the 1964/5 New York World's Fair.

Meanwhile, Rolly Crump had continued to work on individual items that he had hoped would act as set dressing in the mansion's interior. A haunted grandfather clock, an animated man made entirely of burning wax, man eating plants and a speaking, articulated armchair were all designed to enhance the mansions creepiness. Walt was impressed by these disturbing designs but didn't feel that they would really fit with the direction that the ride was now taking. He did however want something at the end of the ride rather than just depositing guests out into the sunshine, so after rejecting the idea of a haunted restaurant Walt suggested that Crump's ideas be collected into a Museum of the Weird, where guests could spend as much time as they wanted looking at the unusual artefacts. A magical gypsy travelling wagon would be the Museum's centrepiece. It would be alive with animated sections, moving paintings and panels, weird lights and flames and mysteriously blowing canopies.

While Crump's Museum of the Weird never made it to production, the rest of the attraction was eventually coming together. Eleven years after first appearing on a park map the Haunted Mansion finally opened in August 1969 and almost immediately brought record attendances to the park.

Despite enduring numerous changes throughout their development, both the Haunted Mansion and the Pirates of the Caribbean finally took up their well-deserved positions in the Happiest Place On Earth. But there have been many other expansion suggestions that have yet to find a home at Disneyland.

Dixieland

Years after the Haunted Mansion's completion another planned Anaheim expansion, Dixieland, would have physically connected the New Orleans Square and

Bear Country, another Disneyland expansion. Dixieland was to have been a link between the French splendour of New Orleans Square with the rustic wilderness of Bear Country. The Mark Twain audio-animatronic figure that today entertains guests at Epcot's American Adventure would also have been brought in for a new one-'man' show featuring the wit and wisdom of Samuel Clements in one of the Country Bear theatres.

Unfortunately guest polls showed that the name Dixieland was found to have unpleasant connotations. People mentally linked the word with the American Civil War and slavery, themes far too negative for Disney to be associated with. The Song of the South movie is still unavailable to buy in America, which put another dampener on the Dixieland concept as it would have tied neatly into that movie. The entire Dixieland idea was quietly dropped, but one of the attractions that had been planned for it would go on, in a somewhat amended form, to be a big success.

Moonshine Express

Everybody loves the Country Bears, right? Those cuddly critters that sing for the entertainment of the people that visit their little theatre? These highly talented animals were initially designed by Marc Davis for the aborted Mineral King Ski Resort in California's Sequoia National Park. The story concept was that the bears had been woken from their hibernation by the sounds and smells of the humans on the ski slopes, and in the restaurants. They struck up a bargain with the humans whereby the bears would be fed and warmly housed in exchange for their daily performances of mountain music. They would literally be singing for their supper.

When the Mineral King project was abandoned, the Bears moved to Disneyland where they became huge stars. But the cute, singing bears apparently had some less friendly cousins and, back in 1985, they were the ones around whom this planned Disneyland expansion would have been based.

These other bears lived way up in the mountains and while their cousins sang for the tourists, these guys apparently spent their days brewing moonshine whisky. Bizarre as it may sound, this is where the ride part comes in. Guests would be recruited by Disneyland's local sheriff to sit in hollowed-out logs and ride the streams and rivers around the mountain looking for moonshine stills. The really crazy part is that the sheriff was apparently too busy to investigate every illegal still himself, so these regular tourists would be sworn in as deputies and issued with rifles to shoot the stills. OK, so they were light sensor triggering rifles but the effect was the same – float along, point your gun at the still, pull the trigger and watch as the still springs a satisfying leak.

As if that idea wasn't bizarre enough, halfway through the ride the naughty bears would appear.

Obviously they would feel aggrieved at these outsiders dealing a severe blow to their moonshine business, and would feel that they had to defend themselves. To put it simply, they started to shoot back at the boats.

Not too surprisingly the Disney executives decided that they had serious concerns about a boat full of paying guests being shot at by angry – not to say drunken - wild bears. It didn't come as much of a surprise when the Moonshine Express idea was quickly dropped.

One thing that everyone liked from this attraction however was its suggestion of guests riding through a mountain in hollowed-out logs. Suddenly those Song of the South ideas didn't look too bad after all. With the removal of the alcohol and firearms themes, The Moonshine Express was given a movie-themed makeover, with careful emphasis on the animated characters, and the Zip-A-Dee River Run was born. This was of course soon renamed Splash Mountain. The human stars of the Song of the South film, regardless of their race or skin colour, were completely absent in the conversion of the Moonshine Express into Splash Mountain.

But there is a small reference to the previous design in the current ride. As the logs ride high up on the outside of Splash Mountain, they pass a large metal canister, a still, with the words "Muskrat Moonshine" stencilled on its side.

Circusland

Throughout most of the 1970's Circusland was thought to be a certainty for installation at Disneyland. This would have extended the park outside of its then-current berm border just beside It's A Small World. All the show buildings in Circusland would be disguised with striped circus tent awnings, and the entire area was to be festooned with bunting and garish attraction posters, giving the impression that a travelling circus had pitched here.

The main thing that people would immediately notice upon entering Circusland would be Dumbo, the Flying Elephant. This incredibly popular attraction would have been moved from Fantasyland to headline Circusland, guaranteeing a steady influx of guests to the area. Somewhat surprisingly, in its early stages the Dumbo ride wasn't going to feature the little flying elephant at all. Instead guests would have ridden in replicas of the hypnotic floating pink elephants.

A Pinocchio dark ride was first planned for this new expansion Land. Although the entire Circusland concept was never taken forward, the Pinocchio's Daring Journey idea was considered strong enough to survive in its own right, and the ride saw the light of day in Fantasyland itself, finally opening in 1983.

A restaurant built around a comical clown theming would be Circusland's main eating house, and small ride called Mickey's Mad House would take guests into the simplistic black and white world of the Mouse's early cartoons. A merry-go-round for younger guests would also be situated here. Called Circus Parade, it would have featured giraffes, lions and other exotic animals.

The major attraction of the area though was to be Circus Disney. Audio-animatronics would feature heavily in this attraction, which would be similar in design to MGM's Great Movie Ride. The concept was one of taking guests firstly through the outer carnival section of the circus, with cartoon style barkers and booths. Finally the ride would roll into the Big Top itself for an actual circus show, all featuring favourite Disney characters. This open format meant that the Jungle Book stars could appear in a wild animal menagerie section, while headline acts such as the hilarious and calamitous Flying Goofys trapeze show would round out the ride.

Toontown

Disneyland opened its Toontown section in 1993. This is the portion of the park where all the characters supposedly live. Just as those 1950's children had requested in their letters to Walt, it was now possible to look around Mickey Mouse's house as well as visit the homes of Minnie, Goofy, and Donald. The backstory for this particular section of Disneyland is that the park was actually located where it is so that the cartoon characters could get to work easily; they've always lived next door to it. Another version of the story is that Toontown was constructed to house the characters alongside the actual park when Disneyland was built. Walt was building a park for visitors to see his stars, so it was only right that his stars got the star treatment, and naturally he built them all houses in their own inimitable styles.

Whichever, when the decision was made to open Toontown to the public (or Mickeyland, as it was once going to be called), they allegedly just took down the dividing wall.

The Enchanted Snow Palace

Marc Davis was one of Walt Disney's original Nine Old Men, and is a Disney Legend. As an artist he was single-handedly responsible for the design of so many of the iconic female Disney characters. Tinker Bell, Maleficent, Cruella De Vil, and Aurora, the Sleeping Beauty all sprang from his brush. But he was also instrumental in the development of such theme park attractions as the Haunted Mansion, It's a Small World, The Country Bear Jamboree, The Jungle Cruise, and his masterpiece, The Pirates of the Caribbean. As Disney heroes go, they don't come much bigger.

But one of Marc's most beautiful designs never came to fruition. The Enchanted Snow Palace would have taken guests out of the Californian sun and into a world of magic and wonder, an oasis of cool and calm in the middle of the heat and excitement of Disneyland. Set in a building that looked like it had been carved out of a natural glacier, a river of melting ice would have taken guests on a boat ride past all manner of natural creatures in a frozen wilderness. Animatronic wolves, polar bears, penguins, and walruses would have all been spotted as the ride started as a kind of Arctic 'Jungle Cruise'.

The boat would then pass underneath a display of the magical Northern Lights, the Aurora Borealis, and out of the 'real' world. Travellers would enter the realm of the Snow Queen, a land populated by frost fairies and snow giants. After being welcomed by the Queen's handmaidens the boat would eventually enter the throne room of the Snow Queen herself. She was to acknowledge the visitors with a wave of her beautiful, pale hand, and as a parting gift she would cause snow to drift down upon them.

The Enchanted Snow Palace was Davis' idea of giving people a cooling respite from the thrills found in the rest of the park. However this was 1978, and thrills were exactly what theme park visitors wanted. Marc's peaceful vision didn't fit in with the demand for roller coasters and white-knuckle rides, so Disney management reluctantly decided against installing this attraction.

The Ice Palace was Marc Davis' last design for Disney. He went into retirement soon after its rejection.

The Monorail

Even in its earliest incarnation as the Land of Tomorrow, Disneyland's Tomorrowland was to always have featured a monorail. The vehicles designed by the ALWEG Company have been sitting atop the rails at Disneyland since 1959 but consideration was originally given to a system designed by the French Safege Company. In their design the cars were suspended underneath the rail. Movie buffs may recognise this system as the one featured in the futuristic sixties film Fahrenheit 451.

Like its Floridian cousin, Disneyland's monorail has been the subject of many expansion rumours over the years. In both sites there have been many plans to link up almost all the parks and resorts that have been constructed. Even in other proposed American Disney parks, the monorail was usually in the plans.

New Tomorrowland

The problem with labelling part of Disneyland 'Tomorrowland' is that it was pretty much out of date by the time it was built. Even Walt himself occasionally referred to this portion of his park as 'Todayland', while some of his successors even went as far as calling it 'Yesterdayland'.

In the mid-nineties, the proposed cure for this was to change the Land's vision entirely. Instead of attempting to depict a factually accurate Land Of Tomorrow, the redesigned Tomorrowland was to provide a retro view of a tomorrow that never was, a vision of the future seen through the eyes of a country brought up on Buck Rogers and Flash Gordon. By 1998 ambitious plans had been drawn up to make Tomorrowland an imaginary future that never has been and probably never would be. New Tomorrowland (also known as Tomorrowland 2055) was redesigned as a totally fictitious future, hopefully removing the problem of its constantly being outdated.

George Lucas, the creator of the Star Wars series of movies, was to have been involved in a new attraction to be built at Disneyland's futuristic section. This attraction, Alien Encounter, never materialised as part of Tomorrowland 2055, but it would later terrify guests at the Magic Kingdom in Florida with it's scenario of a vicious extra-terrestrial breaking loose from its confinement cell and walking among the restrained audience.

Tomorrowland 2055 would also have included an audio-animatronic musical variety show starring alien musicians that had supposedly landed in California as part of a Galaxy-wide tour. Plectu's Fantastic Galactic Revue, starring the audio-animatronic aliens of P. T. Quantum's travelling band, would have been located in the old Carousel of Progress building. That elderly show's revolving seating around the central stage would have remained intact, but the outside of the building would have been redesigned to look like the gigantic alien ship. The new presentation would involve a series of musical numbers performed by strange audio-animatronic creatures from other planets.

The ambitious upgrade of this part of Disneyland would mean it was also to get versions of some of the attractions that (as we'll see later) were announced for Walt Disney World's Tomorrowland as part of the Disney Decade. The Anaheim park was to get a brand new George Lucas 3D movie and the From Time to Time Circle-Vision 360 film starring the Timekeeper. To fit all this into Tomorrow Land 2055's finite amount of floor space, the entire area would be given a second storey which would be linked to the surrounding buildings by Sky Walks, Perspex corridors in the air.

Unfortunately, budgetary restrictions meant that despite the great new retro décor, most of the planned expansion remained on the drawing board. One of the Imagineers who worked on the project claimed that "Disneyland's 'new' Tomorrowland was in design for two years, complete with attractions, schedules, and budgets before it was turned off. A whole new team was assembled, and with a fraction of the budget came up with what you see in the park today. I believe the original concept was light years better then what actually made it in, but as fate would have it, it never made it to the light of day."

The only innovative new attraction to be produced at this time was the terribly unstable Rocket Rods. This high speed slot car ride ran around a track high above Tomorrowland, but was so prone to breaking down that it was permanently mothballed within three years of its opening. Even worse, no corporate sponsor could be found for the ride, so its planned high speed banked curves never materialised. Its sole attraction was its speed, yet it had to slow down dramatically as it entered the curves on a track that had been designed for a previous, much more sedate, attraction, the Peoplemover. The idea was a good one though, and the high speed banked corners would later emerge as a favourite section of Epcot's Test Track ride.

New Tomorrowland would have supplied a huge injection of new material into 1990's Disneyland. But twenty years previously the company was giving serious thought to an even bigger expansion plan.

Chapter 6 – The Undiscovered Bay

IN 1974, AMBITIOUS PLANS WERE DRAWN UP FOR the largest expansion in Disneyland's history up to that time. It was to be an entire new land, and one whose non-appearance would be lamented by Disney enthusiasts for decades to come.

Discovery Bay would have been a thriving port cut into the banks of the Rivers of America at the north of Frontierland. It was to have been based upon a fictionalised San Francisco of the mid-1800's, a time of dreamers and adventurers, an industrial era of invention when anything seemed possible. Much of Discovery Bay was the brainchild of Imagineer Tony Baxter, who described it as "a once-only place in time; it's a Victorian place that occurred at the turn of the century. It's the kind of place that Jules Verne or H. G. Wells might have inhabited".

This place of exploration, strange tales, and imagination would fit perfectly between Fantasyland and Frontierland, allowing the Imagineers to bring in attractions that were not really fairy tales, nor backwoods frontier adventures, but fell somewhere between the two. Discovery Bay's attractions would fan out around the new river inlet, and its plans would go through many revisions over the years as the Imagineers tried to find a way to get the project accepted by Disney top executives.

An old lighthouse housing a shop and a small maritime display would mark the entrance to the Bay. Guests would be able to climb the tower for a spectacular view of the entire Bay from its viewing platform. The surrounding waterfront would be the Chinatown of the Gold Rush, complete with an authentic Chinese restaurant and a shooting gallery named The Fireworks Factory. This would contain an assembly line of pyrotechnics that could be spectacularly ignited by dead-eyed guests armed with light-beam guns. While the proposed shooting gallery wasn't passed, its name would resurface as the short-lived Fireworks Factory barbecue restaurant in Walt Disney World's Pleasure Island complex.

Another eating house, Appleseed's Cider Mill, was to be the first eatery guests encountered on entering the Bay, while another wonderfully themed fast food restaurant, The Chowder House, was to be based on San Francisco's Cliff House, a famous restaurant destroyed in the 1906 earthquake. Indeed The Chowder House was actually named Cliff House in some versions of Discovery Bay's plans.

Disneyland's grand sailing ship Columbia, a three-masted replica of the first American ship to sail around the world, regularly cruises the Rivers of America to this day. It was hoped that this beautiful ship would find a new home in the waters of Discovery Bay alongside other permanently moored craft, where she would be available for guests to explore.

One of the most striking images of this new section of the park, the icon that would have been visible from across the water, would have been a huge dirigible jutting out of the front of an attraction building. A full-scale model of the Hyperion airship would be seen floating out of its hangar, which would double up as the attraction's entrance and queuing area. The ride that Disney was describing as the focal point of Discovery Bay was to have been based on the then-recently released movie The Island at the Top of the World. Tony Baxter described the ride as "a flight on an aerial suspended monorail system that looks like a dirigible".

Upon boarding their own somewhat smaller versions of the airship, passengers would lift off on a twenty-minute flight to an arctic wilderness which would be inhabited by all manner of audio-animatronic beasts. As the journey began, a magnificent sunset would soon give way to darkness, and the shimmering greens and purples of Northern Lights would appear, an idea which would be reused in the plans for the Enchanted Snow Palace. Due to turbulence and an impending storm, the dirigible would have to fly low over the ocean and icebergs until solid ground was spotted. Polar bears, reindeer, walruses, whales and even a solitary snow leopard would be sighted as the flight continued northwards. Eventually, seeking shelter from the worsening weather, the craft would be forced to pass through a narrow crack in an ice wall. After only just making it through, the travellers would have found themselves in a silent frozen labyrinth, with crystalline walls all around. Could they have stumbled across the fabled lost city of Astragard? An ancient temple made of ice and whale bone would confirm the lost civilisation which, riders would be informed, was explored just once, by a Captain Brieux, who charted it as the gateway to the legendary Island at the Top of the World.

The flight would then continue into a strange but beautiful temperate garden paradise. This lost world was a lush habitat for fantastic creatures, safe from the ravages of man. Griffins, woolly mammoths, dodos and winged horses were all suggested as possible inhabitants of this area. Against the advice of the crew, the Captain would attempt to capture one of these animals, but the conflicting icy and tropical air currents would begin to play havoc with the airship's gentle flight. It would swing wildly up into the raging storm, throwing the passengers around in a rough ride. As if this wasn't enough, some versions of the design planned for a volcanic eruption to disrupt the flight too. Safety would now be the main issue, and all on board would heave a sigh of relief when the Captain managed to manoeuvre the Hyperion through a cloudbank to reveal the lights of Discovery Bay twinkling below.

But there would be one final twist. It would seem that the Captain had been more successful than first thought in collecting one of the fabulous beasts, as at the disembarkation point he would be seen proudly displaying his newly acquired pet, and the Hyperion's new mascot.

This then was to be Discovery Bay's headline attraction, but it was by no means the only ride that was planned for the new park section.

Like the now-departed Skyway in Disneyland, the Western Balloon Ascent was to have provided guest with aerial transport across the park while being an attraction in itself, flying park visitors from one side of Discovery Bay to the other. These hot air balloon gondolas would deposit guests at another proposed new Land, Dumbo's Circus, which would form the link between Discovery Bay and Fantasyland. On the other side, to the south of Discovery Bay, would be another attraction linking Discovery Bay to the rest of the park. The main reason that this fictitious town had sprung up where it did was the discovery of gold in the area around San Francisco. This gold-rush fever was to be represented by a ride that would thematically connect Discovery Bay with the neighbouring Frontierland: a runaway train ride named Big Thunder Railroad.

The 20,000 Leagues Under the Sea movie would contribute greatly to the overall design of Discovery Bay, with a two hundred foot long scale model of the

Nautilus submarine being permanently moored in its waters. Disney's 20,000 Leagues film ended with the Nautilus sinking to a watery grave, but Discovery Bay's backstory had the town's founder and most famous resident, fictional adventurer Jason Chandler, recovering the stricken craft. Chandler had brought it to this secluded area of the San Francisco coastline, where it was now to be permanently berthed, and opened up to visitors.

Upon entry into the mighty vessel, guests would have three options available to them. Firstly, they could walk through the Nautilus itself, viewing the mysteries of the submarine, in much the same way that visitors to Disneyland Paris can do now. The control room, the crew's quarters and of course Nemo's pipe organ would all be available for guests to see.

The second attraction in this area would be a Captain Nemo Adventure simulator ride. Today simulators are standard theme park attractions and even appear at travelling fun fairs, but in the mid-1970's they were so new and expensive that they were strictly used for fighter pilot training. No-one had even considered using them for entertainment purposes before. Then again, no-one else was Disney.

As part of the ride's pre-show, an audio-animatronic version of the actor James Mason as the 20,000 Leagues movie's Captain Nemo would have welcomed guests aboard his ship and shown them into the circular theatre. He would have described it as an experimental submarine, one that was capable of holding a hundred and fifty passengers. As the adventurers began their short journey to Nemo's undersea development, glass containers mounted on the walls would flood with water showing how the vessel was submerging, and lanterns would swivel in their housings to emphasise the angle at which it was diving. Of course, there would also be huge windows offering views of the mysteries of the deep.

After some initial plain sailing viewing fish and watching some of Nemo's men working on the sea bed farm, an alarm was to suddenly ring out. An enemy ship had been spotted and was firing at Nemo's new creation. The Captain would issue the command, and his sub would suddenly accelerate to ramming speed. The subsequent collision would rock the theatre violently as the prototype sub tore through the hull of the opposing warship. Nemo would then turn the ship just in time to see the wreckage of the enemy's ship disappearing beneath the waves. Unfortunately his own submarine would also have sustained some damage and at this point in the show would suddenly lurch out of control downwards, far deeper than it was ever designed to go. The walls would creak with the pressure and emergency lighting would fill the theatre with an eerie glow that would have been compounded by the strange phosphorescent deep-sea fish visible outside. However, Nemo and his crew would eventually regain control and gently ease the ship back into shallower waters. But just as the relieved passengers started to think that their journey was coming to a safe conclusion, there would be one final terror awaiting them.

Without warning, a giant squid would suddenly attack the ship. Although a quick-thinking crew member was to discharge electricity through the hull in an effort to dislodge the creature (causing an impressive display of blue sparks in the cabin), the squid would hold on, intent on tearing the small submarine apart.

The riders would then be told that the only way to destroy it would be to rise rapidly to the surface and hope that the sudden change in pressure would cause sufficient damage to the creature. This would prove to be the case, but not before the squid had managed to tear open an overhead hatch and, as a final surprising thrill, insert a couple of wet, wildly thrashing tentacles into the theatre.

This kind of large-scale simulator attraction sounds amazing but it would be technologically difficult even today. Back in 1976 it would have proved practically impossible.

There was one final area in Discovery Bay based on the Captain Nemo story. Guests could experience some of the finest dining available on all Disney property at the three-hundred seat Grand Salon restaurant. It would allow diners to experience the stunning beauty of the Nautilus' main dining hall, complete with picture windows giving tranquil underwater views of the thriving fish population of the Bay itself.

Jules Verne, the French author of The Island at the Top of the World and 20,000 Leagues Under the Sea was to have provided the inspiration for all of these attractions. In fact Verne was such an inspiration to Discovery Bay that a statue of him would have been erected in the middle of the town square. His vision of grandeur represented in the interior of Captain Nemo's Nautilus would be reflected in the street front facades with their plush interiors and crystal chandeliers.

But it wasn't only the work of Monsieur Verne that provided background material for Discovery Bay.

H. G. Wells' time machine would have been represented by a ride that was at various times referred to as Voyage Through the Fourth Dimension, the Lost World Rapids, Journey Through Time, Travels Through Time, Voyage Through Time, and Mythia – Land of Legends. This would have been a log flume ride similar to the Pirates of the Caribbean but lasting anywhere up to fifteen minutes. The main storyline was simple but extremely flexible; a magical portal through time would allow guests to visit audio-animatronic versions of lost civilisations and let them travel further back to the beginning of time itself. As with the Island At the Top of the World ride, this would have showcased many mythical creatures, including dragons and dinosaurs, centaurs and unicorns. This would suggest that only one of either this or the Hyperion ride would have been constructed, or that had they both been built then at least one of them would have had this section removed.

There was one nice nod to the past in this historical fantasy. If the dinosaur section had gone ahead, the caveman and dinosaur audio-animatronics used would have been fashioned after the ones created by Disney for the Ford Magic Skyway attraction at the New York's Worlds Fair.

This time travel ride went through many different revisions, some with and without a human guide, and some relying more on log flume drops in the dark than others. In later incarnations of the ride the mythical creatures had been removed entirely, but all versions were to have included dinosaurs in some form or other. The time portal arches and dinosaur chase that were mentioned in these plans are very reminiscent of those eventually created in Disney's Animal Kingdom's Countdown To Extinction ride (later renamed Dinosaur when the movie of that name was released) which appeared some 25 years later.

Of course the Disneyland Railroad that circles around the perimeter of the park would have to have been re-routed to include the fascinating world of Discovery Bay. In fact a new stop was planned at the Discovery Bay Station, from where the train would cross the waters of the bay itself via a rickety late nineteenth century wooden bridge. In one of the designs for this expansion the railway track would have fully encircled Discovery Bay, weaving a figure eight loop around its perimeter.

Another new attraction for this exciting new Land would be housed in a patchwork circus-tent. Professor

Marvel's Gallery was to be an update of Rolly Crump's old Museum of the Weird idea, the collection of artefacts featured in an early version of The Haunted Mansion concept. Professor Marvel himself would be an over-the-top showman in the P. T. Barnum tradition, inviting guests to view his strange collection of extinct creatures, freaks of nature and bizarre devices from extinct civilisations, crazed inventors and brilliant alchemists. The presentation would have been similar to Walt Disney's Carousel of Progress, with a circular, rotating theatre turning around a series of audio-animatronic set pieces where the professor would introduce his displays of strange and wonderful exhibits.

There was to have been one more thrill ride in Discovery Bay. The Tower (also known as The Spiral) was to be the power plant of Jason Chandler's town. It was to be a huge pillar pointing to the sky, topped off by an astronomy observatory. Not only would the Tower's design look impressive, but it would also house an indoor looping roller coaster. Known in other versions of the plans as the Spark Gap Electric Loop, this ride was to be themed around the demonstration of a massive electromagnet. This powerful humming and throbbing magnet would pull a roller coaster car up a steep track, and then suddenly reverse the magnetic field, forcing the car into a corkscrew loop through the Bay's power station with electricity arcing and crackling all around.

Discovery Bay sounds fabulous. It would have surely brought in the paying public in droves. A beautiful design model of Discovery Bay sat for years in

Disneyland's 'Previews of Coming Attractions' centre, giving visitors an idea of what the finished article would eventually look like. The company had at one time been so enamoured by the whole idea they seriously considered expanding the Discovery Bay concept from a single Land to become Disneyland's second park in Anaheim, on the plot that was eventually developed as Disney's California Adventure. Unfortunately, The Island at the Top of the World movie that introduced many of Discovery Bay's themes didn't do anywhere near as well as expected at the box office, and interest in the entire expansion waned. Fears were raised that the public might not be quite so enamoured as expected by these tales of exploration adventure, and the whole Discovery Bay idea was abandoned. The land that it would have occupied became the Big Thunder Ranch, housing the horses that work on Main Street USA, and the Big Thunder Barbecue. After a decade as a corral, the site was converted into an outdoor theatre to host The Hunchback of Notre Dame show.

Looking back, Discovery Bay's non-appearance is perhaps understandable. This was the late 1970's, and the new proposal's particular kind of Boy's Own style adventure had been superseded by the space fantasies of the two big smash hit films of the day, Star Wars and Close Encounters of the Third Kind. People no longer wanted lost worlds and dinosaurs, they now dreamed of spaceships and aliens. Had the movie The Island At The Top Of The World been a success however, then no doubt we would have seen many more attractions in

Discovery Bay's style actually making it into the parks. Tony Baxter explained why this anticipated section of Disneyland was never constructed. "Discovery Bay was banking on Island at the Top of the World. We thought this would make our mark in science fiction and put us back in the live action business, but it was a terrible movie. It bombed and it killed Discovery Bay along with it".

That, it would appear, was that.

But in 1985 the idea was quietly investigated again, this time as a possible theme park in its own right. The hope of the Imagineers was that this might have opened its doors in 1988. And in 1998 yet another map was produced showing how the Bay might look in the Disneyland park, this time incorporating the amazing Fantasmic! show into it. Again though, these ideas were rejected and Discovery Bay was never to be constructed.

Although the project was dropped, it hadn't been forgotten about. When EuroDisney was being planned, its head designer was the same Tony Baxter who had drawn up the original Discovery Bay plans. He went back to his earlier designs and integrated many of those ideas into plans for an ambitious section of the new park named Discovery Mountain. Even though this idea too would fall through, Discoveryland at Disneyland Paris today incorporates more than a few attractions whose origins can be traced back to Discovery Bay.

The giant Hyperion Airship that now hovers above the entrance to the Videopolis dining and entertainment hall in Paris would have originally graced the Island at the Top of the World ride building at Discovery Bay. There's also Les Mystères Du Nautilus, an underwater attraction where guests can walk through Nemo's ship and see the giant squid attack the sub. And other Disney parks have also benefited from portions of the Discovery Bay plans too. There are, for instance, some sections of Tokyo Disneysea that could have come directly from the Discovery Bay blueprints.

A short pilot film was made for a potential TV series called The Discovery Bay Chronicles, and there was also discussion of an animated television show. Both of these would have depicted the adventures of Jason Chandler, and would surely have heralded the arrival of this most wished for Disneyland expansion but, like the ill-fated Bay itself, neither of these projects would ever be seen by the general public.

While Discovery Bay may never now be built at Anaheim, the company has made it clear that they intend to build a third theme park at the original Disneyland resort in California. As to what that third park might be, we can only guess. However Anaheim's second park has now been established for quite some time.

Disney's California Adventure

Disneyland has always been seen as the Disney company's flagship park, the park that Walt built, the Happiest Place On Earth. But when Michael Eisner was brought in to run the company in 1984, he quickly realised that it generated only a small portion of the income that Walt Disney World was bringing in on the west coast. There was land available next to Walt's old park. Not much land, it's true, but by moving the car parking area there would be room for another small development and, most importantly from a corporate point of view, a money-spinning Downtown Disney complex complete with more hotels, shops and a night-time entertainment area.

While the impressive but staggeringly expensive Westcot development looked likely for quite some time, the park that was eventually constructed here was Disney's California Adventure. The reception to the new venture was lukewarm at best. Some of the people who worked with Walt on Disneyland were especially hostile towards it, with one famous old-time Imagineer being memorably reported as saying, "I liked it better as a parking lot".

Yet even the Disney's California Adventure that was delivered was somewhat different from the planned version. For example the short lived Superstar Limo ride went through at least two thematic changes before being approved. It might have been Goofy's Limo Service, or perhaps, after the Muppets were brought into the Disney fold, Miss Piggy's Limo Service. A zany dark ride in the manner of the fan favourite Mr Toad's Wild Ride was also considered for a while. Instead the Superstar Limo became a dark ride of a much slower pace, and the timeless Disney and Muppet characters that it was going to showcase were substituted for audio-animatronic caricatures of TV stars and celebrities of the day. Never popular with the public, it was in operation for less than a year.

But all of this was very much in the future. Long before any second park was considered at Anaheim there was a small matter of another development on the other side of the country to be considered.

Chapter 7 – The Mouse Moves East

AFTER THE HUGE SUCCESS OF DISNEYLAND IN Anaheim, it was only a matter of time before an east coast version of the park was built. Walt Disney is frequently quoted as saying that he hated sequels, that he hated repeating himself. He was of the opinion that repeating any business success was lazy and showed a lack of new ideas. Therefore any new venture that he were to embark upon was never going to be simply a replication of the Californian park. Walt was also unhappy at the number of cheap motels and fast food joints that had sprung up around Disneyland. And as much as he disliked repeating ideas he decided that if he were to build a whole new Disney world, then this time he would buy up enough land around his park to keep such intrusions at bay. More land would be needed anyhow, because this time Walt was dreaming bigger dreams. Dreams that included a small airport, a thousand acre industrial park, and even an entire city.

Alternative Sites

Walt Disney had discreetly commissioned a study of possible locations for another theme park in 1959. He wanted his second Disneyland to be near the east coast of America but not actually on the coast itself if it didn't want to suffer from competition with the area's beaches. Baltimore and Niagara Falls were early contenders. St Louis, Washington DC, and Queens, New York were also considered although all investigation was necessarily discreet. This new prospective Disneyland East was a top secret project, referred to by those in the know at various times as Project Winter, Project Sunshine, or Project X, a codename that Walt would later use to refer to his Epcot dream. A large piece of land near the city of Washington emerged as an early favourite location, but once that was rejected the search settled on Florida, with North Palm Beach looking the most likely option.

Miami was already an established holiday destination but it was deemed to be too far south to be a viable site. If they located the new park in the centre of the state then not only would it be easily accessible from all directions, but it was hoped that holidaymakers on their way south might make a short-stay visit also. That ruled out Daytona Beach, so sites near Orlando became the most desirable. Once the location had been decided, "Master Plan #7", drawn up by Imagineer Marvin Davis, was selected as the final grand design for the Florida Project.

One thing that was lost from translating Walt's original sketch for Disney World to a working plan was an area he had earmarked for a Swamp Ride. His thought was that a large section of the Florida property would be left as natural swampland. For an extra fee guests could board airboats and be escorted around this natural wilderness. This idea has been reconsidered a few times since then, but the feeling now is that the area has been developed so much that there isn't any real Florida swampland of any size left in the immediate vicinity. It would mean transporting guests some distance away from the parks.

The Magic Kingdom

Sadly Walt never got to see his Disney World completed. He died in 1966, leaving his elder brother Roy to come out of retirement to ensure the project's completion. In building Walt Disney World, which he had insisted be renamed as a tribute to his late brother, Roy Disney tried to make the Magic Kingdom park as close to the design of Walt's original Disneyland as possible. He generally got his wish, however the design team had wanted to replace some of the dark rides from Disneyland. Had they got their way then Snow White, Peter Pan and the Mr Toad ride would all have been dropped and in their place three new dark rides would have been commissioned. Rides based upon Sleeping Beauty, Mary Poppins and the story of Ichabod Crane and the Headless Horseman all went through varying stages of design before being abandoned. In fact a Mary Poppins ride had been suggested many times for both Disneyland and its newer Florida counterpart.

The layout of the Magic Kingdom replicated that of Disneyland with its central hub being dominated by the castle and surrounded by different Lands. Some of the attractions are different, but a guest who has visited one park will certainly feel at home with the layout should they visit its opposite number across the country.

Between the Magic Kingdom's Main Street USA and Tomorrowland is a restaurant called the Plaza Pavilion. In the early 1990's this was slated for a total refit from which it would emerge as The Astronomer's Club. This was planned to have been part of a renaming of Tomorrowland to Discoveryland, the name by which the area is known in Disneyland Paris. The Astronomer's Club was to be a whimsical and highly themed dining area where science and technology met in a full service restaurant, a kind of Hard Rock Café for space junkies. It was hoped that scientist and actual NASA astronauts would make technology based humorous presentations while the diners worked their way through their meals. Other guest speakers would have included the likes of Leonardo da Vinci, Galileo, and H.G. Wells. These historical figures would have been brought to the club via Nine-Eye and the

Timekeeper, stars of the From Time To Time show which was to have been in the adjacent building.

Another feature of the Magic Kingdom's Discoveryland was to have been a resurrection of an old Disneyland favourite. The Carousel of Progress building was to have been gutted and used as an arena for the innovative but highly unreliable Flying Saucers. These personal hovercrafts had operated for a few years at Anaheim but had fared badly outside in the heat of the Californian sun and were forever breaking down. They would, it was hoped, have performed much better given protection from the weather in the Carousel's circular building.

In 1988 the America Sings attraction had vacated the Carousel Theatre that had originally been home to the Carousel of Progress. The unusual revolving theatre was then slated to host an attraction named The Greatest Moments In Disney Musicals. This would have presented audio animatronic performances of famous songs from Disney classics on the theatre's stages while the audience rotated from one diorama to the next. The suggestion was that the movies represented in the show could be changed as public demand dictated.

This idea was later adapted into plans for a Fantasyland dark ride with numerous musical scenes. The design of this ride was abandoned too but the thought wouldn't go away and eventually it became the inspiration for the Great Movie Ride at the Disney MGM Studios.

The issues of how to replace a much loved attraction like the Carousel of Progress were repeated over the 20,000 Leagues Under the Sea submarines. When the dated underwater fleet was removed from Walt Disney World in 1994 it was clear that a major replacement headline ride was needed. Two separate Imagineering teams produced similar roller coaster concepts and, for a time, both were given quite serious consideration.

Fire Mountain would have been situated either in the 20,000 Leagues Lagoon or as part of a new expansion behind the Pirates of the Caribbean ride. It would have reused yet another old idea that had first been suggested for Discovery Bay, that of having a roller coaster set inside a volcano. If everything had gone to plan, Fire Mountain would have started off as a regular ride with guests sitting on top of the ride mechanism. Then halfway round, as the volcano erupted, the entire car would drop sickeningly through the tracks to swing freely underneath. In an instant the ride would switch from a seated to an inverted coaster with the guests suspended beneath the track as it built up speed. This was to be a serious "E-ticket" attraction, with at least three loops and even a simulated 'underwater' section. The speculation was that this attraction could have been operational in time for Walt Disney World's 30th anniversary celebrations in 2001. However much of its planned theming was possibly going to be tied into the animated movie Atlantis, which ultimately proved to be relatively unsuccessful at the box office, and the Fire Mountain development has so far not been carried forwards.

The other design considered for the abandoned lagoon was Bald Mountain, a log flume ride based on the Chernabog demon section of the Fantasia movie. Its similarity to Splash Mountain however is undeniable, and this in itself made it unlikely to be constructed at the Magic Kingdom.

But if Bald Mountain (or Villain Mountain, as it was also known) wasn't to be built over at the Magic Kingdom, it would have fit perfectly inside another proposed theme park.

Shadowlands

Shadowlands was an idea for a possible fourth theme park on Disney's Florida property. This initially small scaled venture was to have appeared before Disney's Animal Kingdom, and would have been themed entirely around the Disney Villains.

The idea started out with the Bald Mountain indoor log flume that had been designed to be built in the disused 20,000 Leagues Lagoon. Then it grew to be an entire dark Magic Kingdom Land stretching away to the back of Toon Town. There is little confirmation as to what exactly would have been in Shadowlands, but a 'Dumbo' style ride themed around Ursula, the Sea

Witch from the Little Mermaid, might have been constructed there before eventually finding a home at Tokyo Disneyland.

The obvious headliner for this area though, either as a land within the Magic Kingdom or as a park in its own right, was the Mountain. Guests would board longboats reminiscent of those on the river Styx in the Hercules movie, and would journey into the depths. Once underground they were to inadvertently interrupt a convention of all the great Disney Villains who would chase the boat through the mountain, intent on apprehending the intruders. Both film and audio-animatronics would have been used to bring these evil characters to life, and of course the only way out to daylight and safety would be for the guests to ride their boat over a waterfall...

Big Thunder Mesa

The Pirates of the Caribbean ride had been successfully launched at Disneyland as part of its New Orleans Square, and it would have seemed sensible to repeat the winning formula over in Florida. However Walt Disney World is a lot closer to the real New Orleans depicted in the ride than Anaheim is, so it was decided not to install a copycat version of the Square in Orlando. Many Floridian visitors would already be familiar with the Big Easy, and Disney didn't want to run the risk of their version comparing unfavourably with the party city. But if pirates had seemed exotic to Americans on the west coast, maybe the eastern park visitors would feel the same way about Wild West cowboys?

With this in mind, senior Imagineer Marc Davis produced a concept based around an old western mining town that he called Thunder Mesa. The main headline attraction of this new Magic Kingdom land would be The Western River Expedition, a raft ride which would follow a Lewis and Clarke style audio-animatronic adventure and would hopefully have opened at Walt Disney World in 1974.

While starting off gently in the Florida sunshine, the river would soon flow into the darkness of a huge mountain. Having much of the attraction indoors would allow all kinds of scenarios to be acted out as the Western River Expedition riders sailed past. Guests might happily view animal figures feeding, or stalking each other but before too long the river would turn a bend and encounter a battle between Cowboys and Indians. Just when it looked as though the raft riders would become involved in the fighting, the river would plunge down a small waterfall and, after a white water section, deposit guests into the bustling Western town of Thunder Mesa. This new section of the Magic Kingdom would even have its own railroad station.

Curving around the mountain on the outside of this show building was to be a runaway mine train ride, which would provide the benefit of two attractions being built within the same space in the park. This mine train was to become the Big Thunder Mountain Railroad, and a young Imagineer named Tony Baxter was given the job to model it. It became such a successful design that Baxter expanded it into the whole wonderful but ultimately doomed Discovery Bay concept.

As we know plans change, and Pirates of the Caribbean was eventually back on the agenda for Walt Disney World. The Thunder Mesa concept was removed, but the runaway train portion was deemed perfect for installation. The fictional Thunder Mesa design gave way to a Monument Valley theming, before finally taking on the look of Bryce Canyon, a feel that fit better with the trees and theming already in the area.

As an aside, it's interesting to see how raft rides have been an Imagineering staple at various Disney parks over the decades: The Western River Raft Expedition, the Lost World Rapids and Cascade Peak at Disneyland; Westcot and Port Disney might have included raft rides, and there have been discussions regarding a possible Brother Bear river voyage adventure to be installed at the Canada Pavilion at Epcot. This is in addition to the Kali River Rapids and Grizzly Peak rides that were actually built at the Disney's Animal Kingdom and Disney's California Adventure respectively, and of course there are the many smaller raft rides at the Disney water parks in Orlando. Even though Cascade Peak at Disneyland was eventually built, it was simply a small decorative mountain island with a waterfall running down its side, a far cry from the water ride that was planned.

Another possible later addition to Walt Disney World's Frontierland was Geyser Mountain, a sort of natural extension of Big Thunder Mountain. The basis of this was a ride on the drilling machinery that supposedly made the tunnels for the Big Thunder Mountain Railroad trains to run through. After trundling through some amazing underground caverns and past bubbling pools the ride eventually was to run onto a very unstable rickety old bridge. Of course, this being Disney, the bridge would sag and rock alarmingly as the vehicle reached the middle of it. Just when it looked as if the mining machine would slip off and plummet into the depths of a vast cavern, riders would hear a tremendous rumbling deep within the earth. The car would suddenly be launched upwards out of the dangerous cavern, propelled into the sunlight at the top of a massive geyser eruption, to land safely on the surface. Using technology similar to that of the Tower of Terror ride and combining it with a huge upward jet of steaming water, this would have been a major attraction.

This new expansion area would have changed the face of the Magic Kingdom forever, had it been built. But we're still waiting. Big Thunder Mesa with its headline rides and Frontierland-style mining town was destined to become one just more great Disney Land that never was.

Chapter 8 – One Man's Final Dream

EPCOT – THE EXPERIMENTAL PROTOTYPE CITY OF Tomorrow – was Walt Disney's last and grandest dream. It was the main reason that he had even considered building an operation on the west coast in the first place. He called it "by far the most important part of our Florida project". Even as he lay in the hospital fighting the lung cancer that would eventually kill him, he was still explaining the details of his dream community to his visitors. He wanted his final gift to the world to be nothing less than the solution to all of man's social problems.

And Epcot is there in Florida today, anyone can go and enjoy its delights. But the Epcot Center that was finally opened some sixteen years after Walt's death was to become 'just another' playground, a vastly different place from the utopian city that the company's chief dreamer had originally conceived.

Walt's Experimental City

At a press conference held to announce the company's plans for Disney World, Walt was asked where all the new people that would be needed to work at the massive proposed theme park were going to live. He responded by describing a small community that he intended to build near to the new development. He explained that Disney World was to include a huge man-made lake, and that the earth excavated to create this lake would be formed into a mountain. And inside that mountain would be a rest area where Disney Cast Members (as employees are called) could relax, wash, swim and even take a nap between shifts. But that was only the beginning. Walt went on to astound the world's press as he described a much bigger idealistic city that he also intended to construct. Within the walls of Disney Imagineering, this new city had become known as Project X, and this was Walt's real Florida dream. For him, the 'second Disneyland' was only the attraction that would bring people in to see his model city. For Walt, the Magic Kingdom was repetition, a financial necessity. Building Epcot, now that would be real progress.

Project X (AKA Progress City) would have been an actual city where people lived, worked and played, but a city more advanced than any the world had ever seen before. It would have been built in concentric circles around a central thirty-storey hotel. Its commercial centre was to have been surrounded by high rise apartments, followed by a ring of greenbelt land. Suburban housing was to form the outer circle of Progress City. Most impressive of all, the entire downtown area at the city's heart was to be covered in a huge transparent dome to protect it from the worst of the extreme Floridian weather.

The radical design of this original Epcot concept was intended to solve many of American society's pressing issues of the day. All service roads would have been hidden from view in underground tunnels, and the residents would only be able to travel into the city via public transportation. This would be on clean and reliable electric vehicles, the monorails and the WEDWAY People Mover that would eventually be seen in Walt Disney World's theme parks. In Walt's ideal city they would mean that inhabitants and guests would be required to leave their personal cars in secure parking at the outskirts of Epcot, totally removing the car from the city centre. These parking structures would have to be huge, as Walt envisaged that this Experimental Prototype City Of Tomorrow (which rapidly became renamed Experimental Prototype Community Of Tomorrow) would house up to 20,000 inhabitants. While some of these would find jobs in the theme park, many others would work at Epcot's proposed industrial quarter. This too would be open to the public, allowing visitors to see behind the scenes at the research and development labs of Epcot's specially invited partner companies.

Almost thirty years later the Disney Corporation would actually design and build its own residential area, the town of Celebration near Walt Disney World. But that small town with its picket fences and neatly mown lawns is no gleaming City of Tomorrow. Instead it's a gentle mix of past, present and future. It's almost an homage to the kind of perfect suburban town that was only ever seen on television. But while externally the homes may appear to date from the post-war years, their interiors are as up to date as any in the world. The houses at Celebration have the latest advances in home technology and the town has some of the most modern health and education facilities in America. It's a remarkable settlement, but it's a far cry from the futuristic vision of the original Epcot.

Even while Disney World was starting construction, Walt's energies were being channelled into planning his new city. At that 1966 press conference he said that Epcot would be "like the city of tomorrow ought to be, a city that caters to the people as a service function. It will be a planned, controlled community; a showcase for American industry and research, schools, cultural and educational opportunities. In Epcot, there will be no slum areas because we won't let them develop. There will be no landowners and therefore no voting control. People will rent houses instead of buying them, and at modest rentals. There will be no retirees, because everyone will be employed according to their ability. One of our requirements is that the people who live in Epcot must help to keep it alive."

Imagineer Marvin Davis later expanded on this. "It was his philosophy not to build a city that would solve all the urban problems all over the world, but to give a chance to American industry to experiment and show to the world just how the problems of traffic and housing could be solved. It would be a place not only for testing physical things but educational developments and all forms of communication. He was greatly interested in solving the young adult problem that faces everybody. If we can successfully show to the world an area in which teenagers are properly controlled and given an opportunity to express themselves and are kept occupied, this is something we really want to work on. So the amusement park as really a secondary thing. He was interested in solving the urban problem. It's a big scope, but that's exactly what he was thinking."

Along the many newsworthy quotes that Walt gave on the subject, he described Epcot as being "A living blueprint of the future where people actually live a life they can't find anywhere else today." Amazingly Walt also suggested that he had ideas for a second city that would be "built specifically as an experimental laboratory for administering municipal governments."

In October 1966 Walt made a promotional movie, presenting the delights of this upcoming urban paradise to potential backers and corporate partners. It was also shown to Florida resident's groups to give them some idea of the massive proposed changes coming to their state.

Unfortunately, we'll never know how much of that original plan would actually have made it to construction as, on December 15th 1966, just ten days after his 65th birthday, Walt Disney died. This hit those outside his immediate circle especially hard as no details of his illness had been released. Although he had looked frail and unwell in his final public appearances, very few people were aware that he had lung cancer and had already had one lung removed.

Economic Reality

After Walt's death, the entire Epcot idea was put on hold. The problem was that nobody knew exactly how he intended to progress with the project. All they had were the notes, sketches, models and the thirty minute film introducing the concept, which was to be Walt's last celluloid appearance. It showed viewers what he planned for Epcot, but didn't explain how he intended to achieve it. It took almost a decade before Disney President Card Walker finally decided to go forward with the idea, and by then the Epcot concept had changed dramatically. The entire idea of a city had been removed, but the spirit of that idea remained.

Long serving Disney CEO Michael Eisner was convinced that this initial experimental city design would have been amended over time anyway. "Had Walt Disney lived I'm sure that Epcot would have evolved, just like everything else he worked on", said Eisner. "It would have changed. What he left behind was just the first expression of an idea that he didn't have time to follow through on".

A 1969 press release from the company stated that "Epcot is designed to respond to the needs of people by providing an international forum where creative men and women of industry, government and the arts can develop, demonstrate and communicate prototype concepts and new technologies, and their application in creating better ways of living." This could still have fit within Walt's utopian ideal and indeed, by the mid seventies a think-tank was created to show just how this was to work.

Two sentences that Walt had spoken in that promotional movie were used to shape the development of the new Epcot: "Epcot will take its cue from the new ideas and new technologies that are now emerging from the creative centres of American industry… Epcot will always be a showcase to the world of the ingenuity and Imagination of American free enterprise". The Epcot promotional movie also referred to "Shopping areas where stores and whole streets recreate the character and adventure of places 'round the world".

If the Disney board couldn't provide an experimental, prototype city of tomorrow, at least they could present the technology that would have been presented in Walt's ever-changing city.

In 1974 a plan was unveiled for a retail expansion to Walt Disney World which it was hoped would be built around the Contemporary Resort near to the Magic Kingdom. While this idea was pretty swiftly rejected, a subsequent plan to take Walt's idea of the showcase for both the world's highlights and technological marvels was further developed. The plan for the new scheme, to be titled Interworld, mixed both of these ideas in one large park, with elements on both land and water.

By the following year the designs had progressed enough for a presentation to be held at the Contemporary. The Interworld name had reverted back to Epcot, and this presentation showed for the first time that at least a part of the Epcot design had evolved into a World Showcase. A model was shown which featured two linked horseshoe-shaped structures in a large figure of eight, each loop divided into a number of areas representing different countries of the world. These segments were referred to as pavilions. To show that each country was equal, they were all allocated the same amount of frontage space, though crucially, the actual footage available behind these fronts varied enormously. In a nod back to the 1964/65 World's Fair, the area where the open ends of these horseshoes met would feature a large structure resembling the observation towers that had been so memorable at New York's Flushing Meadows. This design showed the World Showcase as a separate park on the Seven Seas Lagoon between the Polynesian and Contemporary resorts. The Future World section of Epcot was not in the plan at all at this stage. This was to have been added at a later date once Epcot Center's World showcase was opened and established.

In announcing that Epcot was finally going ahead Disney's then-CEO Card Walker explained how, while Walt's idea of an actual city was no longer viable, the company were going to produce what Walker called "The Epcot concept".

The new objectives were to create a place where new ideas could be fostered, new technologies, ideas and systems could be developed in an environment of enthusiasm and encouragement. While this may have represented the spirit of Walt's Epcot, by this time plans for the residential city had been completely abandoned as unworkable and not economically viable.

Even when the vision of the park had settled into its more or less finalised version, there were still many things amended or removed from the blueprints. For example The United Kingdom pavilion was initially to have featured a Crystal Palace at the rear (where the hedge maze and bandstand were eventually situated), and a 300 seat Edwardian Music Hall dinner theatre, presenting a revue of vaudeville acts.

The Italian pavilion too would have been very different. It was at one time designed to feature gondola rides. While the gondolas were created, they never carried their intended passengers, and they now sit as mere decorative vessels among the striped poles at the Italian waterfront section of the pavilion.

Similarly in Germany there would have been a boat ride, this one down the Rhine river of that country. The night-time ride through the Black Forest went through at least two changes of scenario, one gently taking guests past various German beauty spots, and the other flowing through re-enactments of scenes from Wagner's celebrated opera, The Ring. Although both of these themes were shelved, much of the attraction survived when it was eventually redesigned and relocated to become the Norway pavilion's Maelstrom ride.

One of the biggest changes to the Epcot plans was the introduction of The American Adventure. The earliest designs for this pavilion show that it would not have contained the inspiring and technically advanced audio-animatronic show that we see today, but would have held yet another boat ride, this one featuring characters from American folk history. The legendary Paul Bunyan and his pet ox Babe would have been seen, for example, singing patriotic songs like Woody Guthrie's This Land Is Your Land.

The Japanese pavilion might have featured a new show as well as a thrill ride which still gets mentioned as a possible addition to the park. The show was to have been a version of Tokyo Disneyland's now defunct Meet The World show, a combination film / audio-animatronic presentation of Japanese history and heritage. This was presented in a revolving theatre much like the Carousel of Progress, but in this instance the audience sat in the rotating centre portion of the theatre while the static outer ring contained the screens and stages.

As for the longed-for ride, that would have been a Matterhorn-style roller coaster to be built in the rear of the pavilion. Guests would ride in vehicles styled after the super-fast Japanese bullet trains on and inside a scale model of Mount Fuji, which was designed to loom behind the current pavilion buildings. The snow-capped peak would have been a major attraction in an otherwise fairly quiet section of the park.

But while it's interesting to see how the pavilions of Epcot's original World Showcase designs differ from the ones we've come to know, it's even more eye-opening to look at those pavilions that never made it off the drawing board.

Additional Countries

Ever since Epcot's opening there have been talks held with various countries and regions to include new pavilions in the World Showcase. It's no secret that a presence at Epcot can be a powerful marketing tool for a country's tourism industry. In 1979 Disney announced that the initial group of ten countries to be represented in the World Showcase would include Mexico, Canada, Japan, West Germany, the United Kingdom, France, Italy and Morocco. With the slight amendment of West Germany being represented by a single united Germany pavilions, these eight nations' areas were eventually built pretty much as intended. But there were two other countries announced in that initial list that were conspicuous by their absence on opening day.

The United Arab Emirates pavilion would have concentrated on the educational contributions that this region has made over the centuries, especially in the fields of mathematics, astronomy and navigation. This would have been highlighted by a magic carpet ride, featuring a holographic genie who would talk guests through the mysteries of the night sky. Remember that this was back in 1979, well before Disney's Aladdin movie, so there would be no Robin Williams craziness from this particular genie.

The second of those initially announced pavilions would recur later in Epcot's history. A plaque marking a 'Future Site' was displayed in the World Showcase advertising an upcoming area where "The Old Meets the New in The Land Of The Bible". A quiet olive and cypress garden would have formed the centrepiece of the never-built Israel pavilion, complete with a small amphitheatre for live performances and a welcoming courtyard containing a large menorah. But the uncertain political situation in that particular part of the world brought security issues to the fore and the idea was ultimately shelved. However Israel would finally be welcomed into Epcot's global family as part of its Millennium Village. This temporary pavilion was part of the celebrations at the end of the twentieth century, and featured smaller presentations from countries that weren't already fully represented in the World Showcase.

One pavilion that seemed certain to appear was to have been representative of a combined Equatorial Africa. A model of it was even featured in the 'Epcot Center – The Opening Ceremonies' TV special in 1982. The programme's host, actor Danny Kaye, told viewers that the new expansion would open between China and Germany in about a year. The major attraction that would have had visitors flocking to this pavilion was to have been a savannah filled with various African animals. Guests could safely watch them from a viewing platform fixed some sixty feet above the ground in the branches of a giant tree. Unlike the Kilimanjaro Safaris attraction that would open much later at Disney's Animal Kingdom though, this attraction would have a twist; the animals weren't actually there. They would have been on film, projected onto a floor-level horizontal screen. Guests would look down on them from their high vantage point and, when the film was combined with surround sound and authentic aromas, the illusion of looking through the foliage down onto an actual watering hole would be complete.

The big theatrical production of this area would have been the Heartbeat of Africa show, a celebration of song and dance from that great continent housed within a large thatched hut. Tribal instruments attached to the walls would play themselves in the same way that the Tiki Room gods drum and flowers sing.

Upon exiting this show, guests would be able to walk through the Sound Safari, a series of pathways filled with unseen dangers. The idea of this was to give intrepid visitors an idea of what it would be like to walk through a part of Africa with its wildlife just out of site but very much within hearing distance. The surrounding foliage would rustle as nearby elephants seemingly lumbered past. Hyenas would laugh, hippos would grunt, all apparently hidden by the plants along the side of the walkways, but still frighteningly close. As a terrifying finale, guests would be required to walk through a pitch black cavern: a cavern in which, so the sounds would indicate, a pride of hungry lions were savagely devouring their kill. It was not for the faint hearted but test set-ups indicated that it would have been very effective.

Africa Rediscovered would bring to life the continent's cultural history, and would have been presented by best-selling author of Roots, Alex Haley. Haley himself was heavily involved in the writing of this attraction, a fifteen-minute film which would have focussed on Africa's history of great civilisations and warriors, including a stunning recreation of the Carthian ruler Hannibal leading his elephants over the Alps.

Sadly Epcot's Equatorial Africa pavilion never appeared, and the only indication today of what might have been is the Africa Outpost. All that was ever constructed of this intended expansion is a simple canopied store.

Another proposed land was Spain, and once again there was a 'Future Site' sign in the mid-1980's saying that the pavilion was on its way. The Spain pavilion would include a travelogue film showing the beauty of the country, a look at the area's arts and passionate culture. The plans also called for a waterfront tapas restaurant to have been featured in this new pavilion to be located between the Germany and Italy pavilions.

Russia and Switzerland were also to have developed their own areas in the World Showcase during Michael Eisner's proposed schedule of theme park expansions during the 1990's called the Disney Decade. Venezuela and Australia were also considered for representation, and more recently Korea wanted their own pavilion. Disney decided against it though, claiming that the Korean's cultural suggestions were too similar to the ones currently represented at Epcot by Japan and China.

One final pavilion to be considered for the World Showcase was not to have been based upon one single country but on the idea of national cuisines. To take one example Imagineer Herb Ryman created a House of Cheese to show the variety of cheeses that are available around the world. Following this idea many countries that hadn't previously been featured in the World Showcase could have been represented at Epcot through their national dishes.

Of course all these possible expansion plans pose a question; If every country that was proposed for inclusion as a World Showcase pavilion actually built one, would there be enough space around Epcot's central lake? There is only a finite amount of waterfront available, and the World Showcase is only one half of Epcot.

Future World

While Epcot's World Showcase themes its pavilions around particular geographical locations, Future World has always presented its ideas in pavilions based around one idea. The Living Seas, The Wonders of Life, The World of Motion, Journey Into Imagination, and others have been designed to make visitors think about their world and how they might make it a better place. This idea was there from the start as the four original pavilions planned for Future World were to have been Life and Health, Seas, Transport and Space.

The Seas pavilion was to have had a very different theme to the one it eventually ended up with. Until the 2006 Finding Nemo overlay it was designed around the concept of an underwater scientific community called Seabase Alpha. Underwater lifts known as Hydrolators carried guests deep down to the ocean floor where they could see all kinds of marine life and watch divers working in tanks among the fish and corals.

Originally, instead of the Seabase Alpha theme and its Hydrolators that visitors to The Living Seas have become familiar with, guests would have entered through a large cave where Poseidon, the Greek god of the sea, would send a huge storm so powerful that it would actually move the cavern's walls. In this way the Lord of the Seas could direct his visitors deeper into the exhibit. He would then serve as narrator for a much longer ride-through section of the pavilion, talking guests through all the beauty of his underwater kingdom from a continental shelf to the Great Barrier Reef.

By the time this submarine section of Future World opened in 1986, it had been renamed The Living Seas. The entire Lord of the Seas concept had been dropped and replaced by the 'scientific' Seabase theme.

The Horizons pavilion has long gone from Epcot's Future World, having been replaced by the thrilling Mission: Space, but like all the other pavilions, Horizons went through a few changes before it finally opened to the public. It was originally to be called Century 3 (or Century III), in reference to America's third century of national independence. The original concept was drawn up in the late 1970s when the Bicentennial celebrations were still fresh in America's memory and the ride's vehicles were designed to fly guests on a "Journey to Century 3". The attraction's name was amended to the unattractive Futureprobe for a brief period, before Disney and their General Electric sponsors agreed on Horizons. Its original idea of space exploration was expanded to champion the broadening of man's horizons on the earth and under the seas as well as towards the stars.

At one time this part of Epcot was simply known as the Space pavilion. Like Mission: Space years later, this would simulate a starship ride away from planet Earth, complete with a zero gravity effect. Celebrated writer Ray Bradbury was involved to ensure a degree of authenticity for this attraction.

The Space pavilion would have held multiple attractions including a space walk, where individual riders would be strapped into their own jet packs which they could, to a degree, control themselves. They would travel suspended beneath a track, effectively floating above a space station. By firing little motors guests would be able to turn to face in different directions, while always gently moving towards the 'safety' of the space craft.

The Life and Health pavilion which eventually became the Wonders Of Life opened seven years after the rest of Epcot after a total of eleven years in the planning. It was to have been headlined by an amazing ride through the complex inner workings of human beings named the Ride Through the Body (also known as The Incredible Journey Within). This was a sedate Spaceship Earth-style peoplemover ride which took visitors along the path of the bloodstream until inevitably passing through a 40 foot tall, steadily beating model human heart.

Its chief designer, Frank Armitage, spent ten years working on this ride, during which it evolved many times. Large working models of the heart and lungs were prepared for the ride, which was for some of its development life to be a water ride along the bloodstream. In yet another set of plans guests wouldn't travel at all, as the presentation was to be given in a theatre in the round. All these versions told the same story though - how our bodies work. It was a fascinating idea born in a time before television and movies graphically depicted the insides of a human body. It would have summed up what Epcot was aiming for, to be both educational and entertaining.

Ride Through the Body was eventually dropped in favour of Body Wars, a thrilling simulator ride based on the movie Fantastic Voyage. This again had guests travelling through a person's body, but this time only on film. Ironically Armitage, who had worked so long on the abandoned project, had done much of the design work for the Fantastic Voyage movie in the 1960's.

There were also plans in the Life and Health pavilion to build a casino-style section that would present information on health and nutrition. This fun part of the pavilion was to have been titled You Bet Your Life, and would show how what we eat affects our overall well-being.

The last of the four pavilions would have been themed around the world of Transportation. Vehicle manufacturers would be invited to showcase their prototype models here, just as eventually happened at the World of Motion attraction. A major highlight at the Transportation pavilion was to have been a ride that allowed guests to safely try out a series of high speed vehicles. Years later the Imagineers would rework this idea into the popular Test Track attraction.

One of the sections of Futureworld that was eventually constructed, The Land pavilion, once again became very different from the version that was originally envisaged. The Land was initially designed to be constructed within seven giant crystals, each one representing a different environmental ecosystem. A visit to The Land would follow the path of water as it falls in the icy mountains, through swamps, woodlands, farmland and urban environments, until eventually finishing in an arid desert landscape where the water would evaporate and the entire cycle would begin again. This was to be viewed in three different ways. Firstly there was an audio-animatronic theatre presentation, next a 'balloon' flight called The Blueprints of Nature which would have taken guests through all seven crystals, and finally a walkthrough section. And the crystal shaped building that was to house the original ecology themed pavilion? This was eventually brought before the public, but by then it was to be the home of the lovable purple dragon Figment in the Imagination pavilion.

Early in the 21st century there was talk of a major addition to The Land. The Rainforest Rollercoaster would have been positioned directly outside the current show building. It was to have been an inverted coaster with riders suspended beneath the track, not seated atop it in the more traditional roller coaster fashion. The plan was to take guests on a ride high up into the forest canopy. It would no doubt have been immensely popular, but the fact that it was considered at all illustrates Epcot's intrinsic problem. The sad truth of the matter is that all the original, worthy, educational ideas haven't proved to be what the public wanted. Generally, people go to a Disney park simply to be entertained. As the pavilions are being upgraded, then this is the direction that the company is apparently going in.

Epcot's icon, the huge 'golf ball' of Spaceship Earth, is due for a refurbishment too. This ride takes guests through the entire history of human communication from cave paintings to the internet and beyond, using life sized animated figures and a stirring voice-over. With the recent addition of a new sponsor, Spaceship Earth's final three scenes are due to be updated, as these are the ones that deal in the communications technology of today and tomorrow. Nothing dates as quickly as a vision of the immediate future.

That might not be all though. There have been plans for an attraction named Time Racers which could replace the existing, slow moving ride. Time Racers would retain much of the current storyline and some of the figures and set-pieces, but increase the excitement factor by the use of time-lapse photography on a high tech thrill ride which would show how mankind is literally racing through time, and how his knowledge is increasing at a phenomenal rate.

One other pavilion was planned for Future World, and it would have been totally different from all the rest.

While most of Future World focussed on technology, science and the power of the human mind, this one would represent the world of Entertainment. In 1985 Michael Eisner had suggested an Arts pavilion, an idea which was soon narrowed down to just focus on entertainment and, specifically, motion pictures.

The entrance to the Entertainment pavilion (also known as the Movie Pavilion) was to have been located between the Land and Journey into Imagination, and would have been fashioned to look like an old-style cinema turnstile, complete with red velvet curtains. One of its earliest planned attractions would have been Mickey's Movie Land, a hands-on, humorous interactive display showing the production of an early Mickey Mouse cartoon. Another idea that got much further along the production route was a show called Great Movie Moments. This audio-animatronic theatre show would recreate memorable scenes from classic live-action movies of the past.

Despite the fact that it looked more to the past and the present than the future and that it would have been quite out of place among the technological marvels of Future World, these Entertainment pavilion plans looked good to the Disney board. In fact, they looked so good that the idea was expanded to become a whole new theme park.

Chapter 9 - The Rest of the World

EPCOT'S PLANNED ARTS-ENTERTAINMENT-MOVIES pavilion eventually evolved into Walt Disney World's third major theme park. After securing a deal with the MGM film studio to use their name, the new park opened as The Disney – MGM Studios. The park that opened its doors to the public in 1989 was greatly expanded from the original pavilion idea, and endured many changes along the way. One thing that has been retained right from the earliest plans though is the idea of an attraction presenting scenes from classic movies using audio-animatronics.

The Great Movie Moments stage show idea that had earlier been planned for Epcot's aborted pavilion was redesigned and became the Great Movie Ride. This slow moving attraction, which takes riders through audio animatronic representations of some of the greatest scenes in the history of the movies, has however been scheduled for a revamp of its own. The updated plan was for the ride to begin much the same way that it always has, but to suddenly be attacked by some of the great Disney cartoon villains. At a certain point in the ride guests would don 3D glasses and see the characters attempt to take over the ride vehicles. Of course, the forces of good would prevail in the end, but not before some close shaves.

The Disney Studios Indiana Jones Stunt Spectacular has proved very popular, as has the Lights! Motors! Action! vehicle stunt show more recently. Before the park was built however, there were two other stunt shows suggested. One of these would have highlighted comedic stunts and slapstick from the era of silent movies, while the other was to have shown huge mechanical action stunts. A further stunt show, this one featuring a younger Indiana Jones, was planned to be developed during Michael Eisner's Disney Decade, but was eventually dropped.

Disney - MGM was also at one time to be the site of one of the Underground Magic restaurants that were proposed by celebrity magician David Copperfield. The walls of these restaurants would be covered with magic props and nostalgia, while close up magicians would wander among the diners, performing slight of hand at their tables. There would also be a stage available for larger tricks. Copperfield had planned a chain of these throughout the USA; indeed much work was carried out on a property near New York's Times Square, a site intended to be the first of the Underground Magic restaurants.

As for the Florida site, a sign sat for a while outside the entrance to Disney - MGM Studios declaring that the combined eatery and magic show would be opening in the summer of 1998. This particular venture never happened, but Disney had better success in a partnership with another star collaborator

Disney CEO and Walt's son-in-law Ron Miller had tried to bring Star Wars supreme George Lucas into the Disney fold with the possibility of a simulator ride themed around his movies. At the time Lucas wasn't interested, but when Michael Eisner took over from Miller as head of the company, he re-established contact with his old pal Lucas. They had worked together on Raiders of the Lost Ark, so as a courtesy Lucas agreed to take a tour of the Imagineering facility in Glendale, California. Eventually the film-maker agreed to be involved in Star Tours, but this blockbuster attraction was originally designed to run for twenty minutes, not the eventual four minutes. Since its installation Star Tours has been a big hit but is now starting to show its age. Plans were drawn up to give the ride an update for the twenty-first century. Instead of the current show with its storyline of a space battle leading up to the destruction of the Death Star, the revamped version would have been based around the pod race from the Star Wars Episode One movie.

A predecessor of Lucas' from the same style of storytelling, Jules Verne has long been a favourite source of inspiration for the Disney Imagineers. When a live action movie of Journey to the Centre of the Earth was being considered in the early 1990's, they needed no further prompting. This time it was to be the Backstage Tram Tour that was to get the Verne treatment, with an additional segment created to take in the Lost City of Atlantis and underground rivers of lava. The passenger tram would narrowly escape an attack by a 30 foot long 'lava worm', and start sliding into the stream of bubbling lava before continuing on its way. Unfortunately the movie was never developed, so neither was the ride extension.

The Rock 'n' Roller Coaster has become a particular favourite at both the Florida and Paris complexes, drawing long lines almost as soon as the parks open their doors. It's a super-fast music themed looping coaster ride featuring one of most successful long-term rock acts on the planet, Aerosmith. But they weren't the first choice as front men for the ride. Originally the Rolling Stones were approached and Mick Jagger and the rest of the band seemed interested initially, but sadly (at least for Stones fans) the deal couldn't be finalised and an Aerosmith overlay was created instead. But just as Aerosmith were not the first band to be considered for this attraction, the Rock 'n' Roller Coaster wasn't the first choice to fill that particular section of Walt Disney World's Disney Studios.

Muppet Studios

Jim Henson's Muppets have provided Disney Imagineering with many ideas for rides, attractions, shows and parades over the years. They were hugely popular in the late seventies and eighties, but as their glory days recede further into the past it seems less likely that we will be seeing any further Muppet-themed expansions at the parks. At one time though they were massively popular; so much so that it seemed sensible to create an entire section of the Disney Studios under the name The Muppet Studios.

This large scale development never appeared at Disney's Florida property, but an even bigger one did.

Disney's Animal Kingdom

Walt Disney World's fourth theme park is like nothing that the company has ever produced before. The park delights, educates and thrills guests with its mix of live animals and the more standard Disney theme park fare. But if the Imagineers' had had it their way, it might have been even more extraordinary.

Disney's Wild Animal Kingdom, as it was originally named, was to have provided guests with a view of beasts from both the natural world and the realm of fantasy, the real, the extinct and the mythical. These mythical creatures would have been housed in an area of the park to be called The Beastly Kingdom. While the Asia and Africa sections of the Animal Kingdom feature creatures of the present, and the Dinoland USA area highlights animals of the past, the planned Beastly Kingdom would have brought guests face to face with the likes of unicorns, dragons, and other creatures that never existed outside the realms of imagination.

The Animal Kingdom's Kilimanjaro Safaris (originally going under the less-than impressive name of Journey to Gorilla Valley) is a major headliner in the park's Africa section. Guides drive guests in large multi-person vehicles on an actual safari through a man-made version of Africa's savannah landscape. Through clever disguising of any artificial barriers, the open vehicles can safely get closer to elephants, rhinos, lions and cheetahs than most people could ever hope. In the case of the giraffes, zebras and gazelles there are no barriers whatsoever, the animals are free to wander right up to the vehicles should they wish, and they frequently do wish.

The final section of the safari though, when guests embark on a bumpy Land Rover chase to halt a group of poachers, is much tamer than it was shown in the first set of plans. As it presented now, the news of the shooting of the female elephant Big Red comes over the vehicle's radio, and guests are pretty quickly assured that she'll be alright. But if it had been produced according to the original concept, this anti-poaching statement would have been much less 'Disney'. Initially the guides and their passengers were to actually find Big Red's bullet-riddled carcass, but minus her highly prized tusks, these having been crudely and very recently hacked out. While certainly doing its job of highlighting the plight of the African elephant, it was thought that this grisly scene would be far too graphic for the average holidaymaker, so now we just hear of the interrupted attack on the radio.

The Asia corner of Animal Kingdom was to have its own water-based safari named the Tiger River Rapids as an equivalent to Kilimanjaro Safaris. While this would eventually open as the environmentally themed Kali River Rapids raft ride, the original concept was for riders to first pass a jungle wilderness where they would see leopards, rhinos, Indian elephants, orang-utans and other animals in their natural habitats along the banks. Viewing them like this would have increased the emotional impact when the river turned a corner and brought riders face to face with the devastating remains of a logging operation. The lush greenery that the raft had just been floating peacefully through would have been totally wiped out due to man's greed. Eventually Tiger River Rapids would pass through a series of deserted and ruined temples which would now have become home to a group of tigers. In this way the ride could show how, given half a chance, nature is able to reclaim man's influence on the land around him. After disembarking the rafts riders would, as now, be able to see more of the tiger exhibit on foot.

At the Animal Kingdom's hub is the magnificent fourteen storey Tree of Life, an impressive but totally artificial tree that has been ornately carved with 325 figures of animals of all kinds. But this wasn't always to be the case. When the park was originally planned its central point was to be an incredible multi-level carousel. At its lowest level would be figures of whales, dolphins and other aquatic creatures in which young riders could sit as they gently revolved along the surface of a pool. Above this would be a more standard carousel with guests seated on horses, rhinos, giraffes and the like. Finally at the highest level of the attraction would be an array of both realistic and fantastic birds alongside other aerial creatures, all carrying guests around the central column like the world-famous Dumbo ride.

It would have been fun, colourful and would have taken three separate queues of guests, but as a central icon for a park it wasn't very awe-inspiring.

A much more impressive ride would have been The Excavator, to be located in Dinoland, USA. This imposing roller coaster would have been situated close to the Bone Yard, the play area where younger children can dig in sand for strategically placed 'fossils'. The Excavator was not intended for these children though. This white knuckle thriller would have taken much older riders through sections of the same bone yard that were deemed too unsafe for the general public due to earth slippages and subsidence. Of course this uncertainty would have played a major part in the excitement of the ride itself.

Beastly Kingdom

When Michael Eisner opened Disney's Animal Kingdom on Earth Day, the 22nd of April 1998 his dedication speech included the following phrase:

"Welcome to a kingdom of animals... real, ancient and imagined. A kingdom ruled by lions, dinosaurs and dragons. A kingdom of balance, harmony and survival. A kingdom we enter to share in the wonder, gaze at the beauty, thrill at the drama, and learn".

Note his words: Imagined animals, and dragons. That would be the same dragon that still appears to this day on the park's logo, alongside an elephant, lion, antelope, and triceratops.

Eisner was alluding to the Beastly Kingdom, a section of the park that was planned from the very beginning and would have been a major expansion once the rest of the Animal Kingdom was up and running. It was to have featured the creatures that never were, that existed only in myth and imagination, and with Disney classics like Fantasia and Hercules to draw upon there were plenty of themes for the Imagineers to explore.

There was so much confidence that the Beastly Kingdom would someday open that parts of it were actually constructed and in place at the park on opening day. As the (now discontinued) Discovery Riverboats sailed circuits around the Tree of Life they cruised past a life-sized figure of Iggy the Iguanodon playing at the water's edge. After passing some mysterious bubbles and eddies in the water they would arrive at the point where Camp Minnie Mickey has since been created. This shaded character meet and greet spot was to have been the site of the Beastly Kingdom. A hint at what was supposed to come could be seen as the boat passed the entrance to a cave at the water's edge. Roaring sounds might be heard, and every once in a while a jet of flame would erupt from the dark gap. This was the lair of a dragon.

These flames and sounds were actually in place for a short while after the park opened. Partially melted suits of armour were constructed to be scattered around the cave's entrance. They were to signify the last remains of knights foolish enough to challenge the dragon. The armour looked very impressive but was never actually installed. They would have later been used for background theming on a ride to be called the Dragon's Tower.

While these sights could be viewed from the water, there is a hint of Beastly Kingdom to be seen from the land too. Looking out into the river from the bridge over to Camp Minnie Mickey there's a lizard made of rocks, as if constructed as a warning of what lies ahead. Most visitors never notice him, but he's in full view and quite large enough to see. Camp Minnie Mickey was just intended as a cheap temporary placeholder until such time that the Beastly Kingdom was given the go ahead. A show built with salvaged and cannibalised floats from Disneyland's old Lion King

Celebration parade was added to the area to try to keep guests in the park for a while longer. To everyone's surprise both it and Camp Minnie Mickey became huge hits with the public and this decreased the chances of the Beastly Kingdom being constructed.

This fantastic Land of the Animal Kingdom was alternatively to be called the Beastlie Kingdomme, with the 'Olde English' spelling added to give it a more mythical, European fairytale ring. Mythical would be the key word here. Dragons, unicorns, and even the Loch Ness Monster would all be brought to audio-animatronic life.

Nessie herself would have been visible at a lake containing legendary sea creatures, called Loch Ness Landing, and at regular intervals throughout the day the eerie sound of bagpipes were planned to be heard floating over the mist-shrouded water. Bubbles would rise in the lake, and mysterious humps would break the surface. Finally Nessie's head would briefly appear before sinking back into the dark depths. Close by the lake there would also be a restaurant, built in the granite slab style of Stonehenge.

A Fantasia Gardens boat ride would carry park visitors through scenes from the movie that merged some of Disney's finest animation with beautiful and moving classical music. The familiar dancing crocodile and hippos would be present, as would fauns, centaurs, and pegusi from those sections of the much loved film. And to add to the feeling of serenity guests would be carried along in boats fashioned like the movie's magnificent flying horses. Upon disembarking, visitors could work their way through a labyrinth called Search for the Unicorn. Also know as Quest for the Unicorn, this was to be a medieval hedge maze with a beautiful, magical, white unicorn sitting peacefully in a water-filled grotto at its heart.

These would be great secondary attractions, but the major ride of the area would be The Dragon's Tower – also known as The Dragon's Keep - a roller coaster inside a ruined medieval castle. Curious guests would be attracted to this area of the park by a crooked tower rising above the ruin which would periodically belch an ominous plume of smoke.

The back story was that the castle was inhabited by some large, friendly and very intelligent bats. These cute, funny audio-animatronics would stand over three feet high and, throughout the queuing area, they would tell guests how an evil, malicious dragon also lived here, and how he had stolen their horde of gold. Would the humans help them rid the Tower of the dragon and reclaim their treasure?

Of course they would. The new willing assistants would be seated in ancient iron cauldrons which would be gripped in the claws of flying bats, their wings spread like a canopy above. This suspended coaster would then take guests up through the dilapidated castle. On the ride soundtrack the bats would be heard encouraging their new-found friends, while also giving ominous warnings that the dragon is aware they are here. Background roaring and some fire effects would increase this feeling of impending menace, in a stark contrast to the humorous set pieces seen earlier in the waiting areas.

Suddenly the ride was to enter the dragon's lair, where all the treasure would be piled high around the snoozing, monstrous beast. As the riders neared, the dragon would awaken. Obviously, having noticed that those annoying bats had returned and this time they'd brought friends, he would be in a bad mood. Rearing up to his full thirty feet he would roar and breathe a ball of fire straight at the cauldron. Up to this point the roller coaster was to have been a fairly gentle affair, giving riders ample time to appreciate the story and set pieces. However now it would be time for a full-speed escape. The ride would have burst out of the castle and flown at full tilt through a wooded area filled with more dangerous ruins, many appearing to be on the brink of collapse. It would have been like the Big Thunder Railroad ride, but through the overgrown castle's remains. The dragon's roar would follow the riders until eventually the ride would return to the safety of the castle's basement where the bats would be urging for just one more attempt at claiming the gold.

This was to be a major attraction, combining an animatronic dark ride with a high speed roller coaster. It would have been one of the highlights of not just the Beastly Kingdom but the entire Walt Disney World Resort.

The plans for the Beastly Kingdom were incredibly detailed, even including small touches like a fairytale Three Billy Goats Bridge, which it was hoped would have had three real goats tethered alongside, and the beautifully designed Mother Goose's Cottage shop. This magical land would have been a great addition to the Animal Kingdom park, but perhaps it was simply too ambitious for its own survival. One Imagineer who worked on the expansion explained, "The funding for Beastlie Kingdomme was at that time part of the [Animal Kingdom's] overall conceptual funding along with everything else. When the park finally got approved to be built, the senior executives took a good look at everything in the park and figured that there was enough there to open it without the huge and expensive Beastlie Kingdomme - and at the same time they saved a huge amount of money. The rumour was that they would add it later, but those of us who worked on it knew that they would never build it to the scale we originally designed".

He was right. Work on the Beastly Kingdom was suspended in January of 1994, four years before Disney's Animal Kingdom opened.

There are still no signs of it being recommissioned.

Chapter 10 - The Disney Decade

AS THE 1980'S DREW TO A CLOSE, DISNEY CEO Michael Eisner made an amazing announcement. He promised the company's shareholders that the 1990's would become known as "The Disney Decade", for in that ten year period he predicted that shareholder income would double. This, Eisner said, was to be achieved in part at least by increased investment in the theme parks. Looking back he was perhaps a little rash in the promises he made, or maybe shareholders were a little naïve to believe it could all be done, but there's no doubting that the developments that were planned for The Disney Decade would have been spectacular.

Eisner's announcement to Disney staff was that the theme park division was about to embark on the largest expansion in its history. There would be massive investment on both Disney's California and Florida theme park sites, with new attractions for every existing park, new resorts, and entire new theme parks to tempt the ticket-buying public with. The Disney-MGM Studios had recently opened and was already proving to be a huge success. Disney was apparently ready to ride the wave of popularity and exposure that this park's launch had brought. It would be, claimed Eisner, "the greatest creative effort in our company's history".

The plans were massive and would have cost billions. Unfortunately, many of these grand designs never came to fruition.

All the Future World pavilions at Epcot were to have been updated as part of the park's tenth anniversary in 1992, and a second musical 3D movie by Disney in collaboration with George Lucas, a companion piece to the Michael Jackson vehicle Captain EO, was also in the pipeline.

Journeys into Space was also announced for Future World. This pre-cursor to the massive spinning simulator Mission: Space went through many different incarnations. At its largest, this new space-themed pavilion was to have included a version of the Mission: Space weightlessness simulator that was eventually produced at Epcot, but instead of being the entire ride, this attraction would have just been the entry point to the pavilion. Once inside, guests would have found themselves on the viewing platform of a three storey space station. They would also have been able to simulate a space walk in a resurrected version of the tracked suspension system planned for Epcot's original Space pavilion. If they could still stomach a meal after that then they would have been able to dine in the futuristic restaurant that was also planned to be sited here.

On the other side of Epcot, the World Showcase was to be greatly expanded too, with the long-rumoured Switzerland pavilion finally appearing between Italy and Germany. This would have included the Matterhorn mountain complete with its very own version of the bobsled ride that is so successful at the original Disneyland. In addition, the world famous onion domes of St Basil's cathedral would rise above another new showcase, USSR.

Incidentally, the Matterhorn has been suggested to appear in three of the Florida Disney parks. This Epcot version in the World Showcase would possibly seem the most logical location, while the most bizarre was the suggestion that it be placed in the MGM Studio park, but be only partially built, like a large piece of movie scenery. The simplest idea was to replicate the Disneyland version in Walt Disney World's Magic Kingdom. This version of the plan however would have seen the Magic Kingdom's Railroad actually pass through the heart of the mountain, with the screams of the Matterhorn Bobsled riders being barely audible over the howling blizzard that the train would have been scheduled to encounter as it steamed through.

Had Eisner's dream come to pass, the Disney–MGM Studios would have also been the recipient of a colossal expansion. Alongside designing the Honey I Shrunk The Kids adventure area and MuppetVision 3D show that were built pretty much as planned, there were also outlines for an entire new area to be named Sunset Boulevard.

Much of Sunset Boulevard was to have been based around the movie Who Framed Roger Rabbit? and would have included at least three major attractions. Firstly there was the Benny The Cab ride, which was eventually developed for Anaheim's Disneyland under the name Roger Rabbit's Car-Toon Spin. Then there was the Toontown Trolley simulator, a large San Francisco style trolleybus with projection screens instead of windows. Unfortunately the trolleybus driver would be none other than the well-meaning but manic Roger Rabbit himself, who would take the ride vehicle on a crazy trip through Toontown.

The final Sunset Boulevard attraction was to be Baby Herman's Runaway Baby Buggy ride, with guests riding in oversized baby carts on a ridiculous journey through the film sets of Toontown Hospital. This would have been based on the Roger Rabbit short Tummy Trouble.

A major ride combining high quality audio-animatronics, special effects and a high speed chase would have been the final addition to the Disney – MGM Studios. Dick Tracy's Crimestoppers was to have appeared midway through the decade. It would have joined the clumsily named Dick Tracy Starring in Diamond Double-Cross show that had already started daily performances at the Studios park and also at Disneyland. Unfortunately the hugely disappointing box office receipts of Warren Beattie's Dick Tracey movie ensured that the ride would never see the light of day and the show itself ran for less than a year.

If the Disney Decade announcements were to be believed the MGM park would have benefited from one more expansion. Mickey's Movieland would have been a nostalgic hands-on interactive replica of the Disney Brothers' original studio from Los Angeles' Hyperion Avenue. This attraction had long been planned, and had even been suggested as an addition to the original Disneyland's Main Street at one point. Sadly, it has yet to appear.

Walt Disney World's Magic Kingdom was to have taken delivery of Splash Mountain, the Timekeeper at the Visionarium, and the frightening Alien Encounter attraction, all of which would please guests at Walt Disney World's centrepiece park. But alongside these attractions would have been One Man's Dream. No, this wouldn't have been the Walt Disney retrospective museum exhibition that appeared at the parks as part of Walt's 100th birthday celebration, but a version of the entertaining stage show that had been running at Tokyo Disneyland for four years.

A dark ride based upon the hit movie The Little Mermaid was also planned for the Magic Kingdom and was initially slated to appear in 1994, although this idea has since been revisited quite a few times. Walt Disney World, Disneyland and Disneyland Paris would all have received their own version of this ride had it gone into production. It's still a favourite concept with the Imagineers which may one day be revived.

As if these additions to Disney's existing three Florida theme parks weren't enough, there was one final surprise announcement. Disney was to build a fourth theme park in the area. This would eventually be revealed as Disney's Animal Kingdom, but that fact wouldn't be announced for another four years. At the time, all Eisner would say was that there would be a fourth park by the end of the millennium, refusing to comment on its theming, but it gives an indication of the size of the investment that he was willing to sign off.

There were also resort expansions planned for the Disney Decade. Fort Wilderness Lodge was built almost as announced (thought the word Fort was dropped from the title), as were the entertainment-themed All-Star resorts. The Boardwalk resort also eventually appeared at Walt Disney World, but in a much altered version to that which had been described. The Disney Decade version of the resort was to have included a small fairground, like a miniature theme park in itself. It would also have featured three dinner shows. One would have been called Family Reunion, which would have combined guests and cast members in one big interactive show. The Disney Magic show would have featured all your favourite Disney characters in a music and magic spectacular. Finally, and biggest of all was Under The Sea, a Little Mermaid themed dinner show set beneath the waves in a massive nine-hundred seat theatre.

Other resorts that were announced but are still to appear were Disney's Fort Wilderness Junction, the Mediterranean Resort and the Kingdom Suites hotel, which was to be built beside the Contemporary.

As if all these new delights on the east coast weren't enough, Michael Eisner was promising big changes over in California too, announcing what he called "the biggest expansion of Disneyland in its history". If all of these changes had come to pass, the Disney CEO would have been proved right. As it was, very few of Eisner's Disney Decade promises actually appeared at the west coast park.

The Muppets would have featured heavily in this Californian expansion. Eisner announced the Muppetvision 3D movie which would eventually entertain guests on both American coasts, but two other Muppet-based attractions never left the drawing board.

Here Come The Muppets was to have replicated the live action stage show that had been running daily performances at Walt Disney World's Disney – MGM Studios. The second announcement was regarding the Magnificent Muppet All- Star Motorcade. This planned daily afternoon parade would have starred all your favourite Muppet characters, including a performance by the Electric Mayhem Band. Had this been successful in Anaheim then MGM at Florida would have got a copy also.

The Disney-MGM Studios was going to become home to a live action stunt show. A show featuring the action and gadgets of James Bond was considered, but they eventually settled on a production featuring Indiana Jones. The show was a great success, so much so that Disney executives gave serious consideration to placing a similar attraction on the opposite side of the country at Disneyland. This wouldn't have starred the adult Jones though. This was to be called the Young Indiana Jones Adventure Spectacular. Had it gone ahead, this stunt presentation would have extended the juvenile hero's mythology in a spectacular series of thrilling adventures, all presented live in the outdoor theatre that would later house Disneyland's Hunchback of Notre Dame Festival of Fools show.

The stunt show would featured a young version of the Harrison Ford character battling various bad guys within a large big top circus tent. As the climax of this 30-minute show, the Magic Kingdom railroad train would actually appear through a curtain and slowly trundle across the set. To the (hopeful) delight of the crowd, young Indy would escape by running across the roof of the travelling train, just as he did in the opening scenes of Indiana Jones and the Last Crusade.

Unfortunately George Lucas' Young Indiana Jones TV series never really found a big enough audience to justify creating a full show, but Lucas had other ideas that were worth investigating, many of which were incorporated into the abandoned plans for Tomorrowland 2055.

Mickey Mouse would also have featured heavily in Anaheim's expansions for the Disney Decade. His 65th birthday would have been celebrated by the opening of Mickey's Starland, a proposed new land which eventually became Mickey's Toontown.

Another whole new section was also planned for Disneyland, to be located between Tomorrow Land and Main Street USA. Hollywoodland would have been an idealised representation of Hollywood Boulevard from the golden age of movies. Much of Hollywoodland would have been the same as the planned expansions for Florida's MGM and was to have included the Great Movie Ride, Toon Town Trolley, Baby Herman's Runaway Baby Buggy Ride and Dick Tracy's Crime Stoppers.

There were also plans for up to thirty new DisneyQuest arenas to be built around the country. The virtual theme parks and showcases for cutting edge video gaming technology were referred to in some versions of the plans as VisionQuest.

Over in Europe Eisner was suggesting that a Parisian version of the MGM Studios might be on the cards. A movie studio park was also proposed for Tokyo Disneyland, but this idea was later dropped and the Japanese park's expansion finally became the astounding Tokyo DisneySea.

And in one final quote, Eisner promised that the development and construction of a second Disney theme park in Southern California would begin before the end of the 1990's.

But the big question was, where would that park be located?

Chapter 11 - California Dreaming

IN THE LATE 1980'S MICHAEL EISNER ASKED THE Disney Imagineers to draw up plans for a new Disney theme park in California. He was aware that guests were spending two weeks or more in Orlando's Disney properties, but only one day at Disneyland. Eisner wanted the west coast Disney fans to spend more time – and of course money – at 'their' home park. As Michael himself said, "There are forty unused acres next to Disneyland planted with strawberries". He offered this fruit field up to the Imagineers for development. In commissioning these plans his brief was simple: "Amaze me".

To their credit the Imagineers did just that, delivering one of the most ambitious plans that the Disney Corporation has ever produced.

Westcot

Westcot was planned to be, as the name implies, a west coast version of Epcot. After years of speculation the plans were officially unveiled during May of 1991. Like its eastern equivalent it was to have had a World Showcase style area dedicated to displaying architecture from around the world. The twist with Westcot was that most of the representative buildings would have been hotels in their own rights. You could, for example, have stayed overnight in an African or Indian themed room at the centre of the park.

The World Showcase would have been much more than a series of glamorous hotels though. The smaller space available at Westcot would have meant that unlike at Epcot, where the countries each had their own individual buildings and areas, here in California they would have to be built together in a series of terraces. Each terrace would have included architecture from more than one country, covering a wide geographical spectrum. These were The Four Corners of the World, showing how all countries are dependent upon on another.

The Imagineers had learned that Epcot guests sometimes felt that the park was more educational than exciting. They wanted to see interesting things, but they wanted to have fun while doing it. With this in mind Westcot would have included more rides and attractions than the park that was its template. For instance the Asian section would have featured The Red Dragon, a steel roller coaster running through the Dragon's Teeth Mountains (though some versions of these plans had it running along the Great Wall of China). Its cars would have been fashioned after the Chinese lion-dragons seen in festival dances. At the point where the coaster would be at its highest, therefore enabling riders to see out of the park, the moving cars would be dramatically engulfed in billowing red and gold silks. This silken shroud would serve the dual purpose of shielding the riders from the outside world, and also bringing an added edge of surprise and disorientation to the ride.

For smaller children there would be a carousel in this area, but instead of the more usual horses, the riders would be seated on mythical Asian animals.

Architecturally the Asian Corner of the World would be composed of Japanese and Chinese elements. Naturally the famous Temple of Heaven and the Great Wall of China would be here, but so would a white marble Indian palace which was to house the dining and entertainment sections of this particular Corner of the World.

The Africa Corner would feature a white water river raft ride down the fictional Congobezi River, as well as an exhibit on the continent's basic farming culture. And of course there would be outdoors entertainment in the form of African drummers. There were also designs to build a grand Egyptian Palace, though this was probably going to have been held over for the park's first expansion.

Potentially the most controversial part of Westcot would have been the headline show in the African section. The Three Great Religions of the World would have been set in a small olive garden and would have shown the Muslim, Christian and Jewish versions of the seven days of creation, with seven of the world's greatest living artists commissioned to depict one day each. The Africa pavilion would have been completed by an art exhibition and The Story Teller Tree, a place where traditional tales would be told and performed just as they would have been in an African village.

A Greek amphitheatre and a replica of the Acropolis would be the central points of the European pavilion. This Corner's headline attraction was to have been a dramatic James Bond-style spy chase train ride aboard the Trans-European Express. This Disney-created train route would have had views of buildings with architectural styles found in Italy, France, England and Germany.

A small region called The Tivoli Gardens would form the entrance to the European section. This children's playground and ride area was named in honour of a Danish amusement park that was a huge inspiration for the way that Walt planned Disneyland.

Also in this European portion of Westcot would be the From Time to Time Circlevision movie / animatronic show (starring Robin Williams as the voice of The Timekeeper) that was so popular at Disneyland Paris and Florida' s Magic Kingdom, and a stage show that had originally been developed for Epcot's abandoned Russian pavilion. Remember, Disney never throws an idea away, though it may sometimes be decades before it eventually comes to life.

The first pavilion that guests would see on entering Westcot's World Showcase would be the Americas Pavilion, with an area representing early 20th century USA at its entrance. In this way the Main Street theming of Walt's original Disneyland would be continued, as the two parks' gateways were to have faced each other across a central plaza. The American Adventure that visitors to Florida will be acquainted with would be here also, albeit in an updated form. The Americas Corner would continue with a Native American Spirit Lodge show in the Canadian section, and an indoor Mexican area which would have included a fiesta show and restaurant. Another spirit show, this time featuring the Inca and Aztec cultures, would round out the Americas section.

There was one final attraction at Westcot's World Showcase. Winding through the entire Four Corners of the World was to have been a boat ride called The River of Time. It would have been the longest ride Disney had ever produced, taking guests on a 45 minute world cruise. It was intended to tour all the external areas of the World Showcase, but with the addition that guests could, should they desire, leave the boat at any (or all) of five show areas. Audio animatronics scenes depicting many of the events shown at Epcot, like Leonardo da Vinci working on the Mona Lisa, the burning of Rome, Michelangelo painting the Sistine Chapel etc would be seen on the ride and the stories begun by them would be continued in the shows. At the end of each performance the idea was that guests could either get on the next boat to continue their River of Time cruise, or leave the show area to explore more of the park on foot.

Westcot's World Showcase would have been a wonderful, innovative update of the Orlando version, not just a copy but a complete update filled with never-before-seen attractions. But that was only half of Disneyland's planned second gate. Just like Epcot in Florida, Westcot would have had its own Future World.

At Westcot's centre was to have been a three-hundred foot high globe sitting on an island in a lake. Whereas Florida's Epcot has the gleaming silver geodesic globe of Spaceship Earth as its icon, the new park's Spacestation Earth would have shone a brilliant gold and been surrounded by a tubular lattice framework. And like most constructions in Westcot, this globe would have contained something fun. The Imagineers had learned that one of the complaints aimed at Epcot was that there was too much 'education' at the expense of fun. For the west coast version they were determined that the entertainment would win out, with guests hopefully learning as a pleasant side effect. The inside of Spacestation Earth was to house an Omnimax theatre that guests would be raised into via an elevating central stage. This film show would have been an uplifting view of mankind's relationship with his world, both natural and technological.

Beneath the incredible web-like sphere of Spacestation Earth would be VenturePort, a natural yet futuristic environment acting as a gateway to the Future World pavilions. Future World was planned to be at a lower level than the World Showcase, with guests reaching it via an escalator. VenturePort would be filled with greenery, mist and waterfalls - some versions of the plans had it enclosed within a giant greenhouse - but once guests passed through this calming zone into the second half of Westcot, everything would be indoors, presented within soundstages to increase the feeling of being removed from reality.

The three pavilions of Future World would have been dedicated to the wonders of the human body, the delicacy of our natural environment and the expansiveness of new horizons. The quote they were using was that this was a place where we could all "Dare to Dream the Future". And these three 'Wonder' areas, when added to the Four Corners of the World in the World Showcase would make up The Seven Wonders of Westcot. Some plans had the Nature and Technology pavilions linked to the VenturePort island via people mover cars that would pass through tunnels under the central lake.

Imagineer Tony Baxter described this version of Future World as being "a lot more participatory, a lot more theatrical. Once you step inside our theater and walk from the audience side onto the stages of Land, Living and Science, we'll ask a little bit more of you".

The Future World Wonder housing The Land would be a two storey pavilion approximately the same size as Epcot's Living Seas. It would contain a horticultural area similar to the backstage tour available to guests at Epcot's The Land, as well as jungle, desert and frozen landscapes to explore. It would also include underwater viewing areas much the same as the Living Seas. One final show in the Nature area would have been the first stop on the River of Time boat ride mentioned earlier.

A nine minute show here would have covered the Earth's history, from the formation of our planet up to the beginning of man's intellectual development. Guests would then be able to get back into a boat continuing over to the World Showcase for the rest of the story, or exit out into Future World.

The Living World Wonder would include a new attraction called Cosmic Journeys. This would be based upon the old Disneyland favourite, Adventure Thru Inner Space, but as well as showing guests their world from a small perspective as Inner Space had done, Cosmic Journeys would also let them grow in the other direction, allowing them to view their whole Universe.

Epcot fans would no doubt have been delighted to hear that the Body Wars and Horizons rides were to be cloned from the east coast, and that a new, expanded version of the ever-popular Journey Into Imagination attraction with Figment and the Dreamfinder would have appeared here too. And of course, at the end of each and every day Westcot, just like its corresponding east coast park, would close with a spectacular fireworks show.

Westcot could have been an absolutely fabulous addition to Disneyland for its paying customers, but perhaps not so good for the people who lived in the area. There were complaints from locals who had seen plans describing the construction of a three-hundred foot tall reflective golden ball in their back yard. Compare that to Epcot's Spaceship Earth, which stretches up a 'mere' one hundred and eighty feet. The Imagineers also tried to envisage how it would look from the Disneyland castle if it could be seen shining over the Main Street Railway Station. Their conclusion? It dominated the skyline far too much, so the Spacestation Earth idea was dropped and replaced as the major icon of the park by a less intrusive (and, it has to be said, much cheaper) huge white spire.

But the expansion wasn't to just be for a new park. The new planned Disneyland Resort would have cost over $3 billion and covered 470 acres, stretching from the original Disneyland park to the old Disneyland Hotel.

Guests would travel from the car parks to the entrance plaza via moving walkways and an elevated shuttle train, while an extended monorail loop would take them from the parks to the Disney hotels. The peoplemovers and monorails would terminate at the seven acre Disneyland Plaza, an open air oasis of tranquillity between the two parks that would be filled with greenery, waterfalls and beautiful landscaping.

Leading from the parks to the hotels would have been an area of shopping and restaurants known as The Disneyland Centre, the design of which would eventually evolve into Anaheim's Downtown Disney area. To one side of this it was hoped that The Disneyland Arena would be created. Referred to in some later plans as The Disneyland Bowl, this would be a five thousand seat outdoor amphitheatre suitable for concerts and other live events.

As well as new hotels that were planned to be built in the style of famous Californian landmarks, there would also be representations of Catalina's Avalon Ballroom and Venice Beach's Boardwalk at the Disneyland Centre. With its emphasis on the varied amount of architecture in the local area, it's clear to see where the idea of Disney's California Adventure came from.

This gigantic expansion was to have been constructed in stages, with the entire resort being finished by 1998 at the latest. It all sounds wonderful, and would have totally transformed Disneyland - had it ever actually been built.

Westcot caused great excitement, and would have been a wonderful addition to the company's collection of theme parks. But there was competition for Disney's Imagineering and construction budget, as another plan for a major development was lined up for another city out on the Californian coast.

Port Disney

While one team of Imagineers were taking Michael Eisner's "Amaze me" edict as their design brief for Westcot, another crew were working on plans for Port Disney, a huge complex to be situated at Long Beach, California. As it was initially announced in July 1990, Port Disney would cover three hundred and sixty acres and include a brand new kind of theme park - DisneySea. DisneySea would have explored man's relationship with the oceans around him in fact as well as in fiction. It would have shown what's really out there under the sea, and what authors and adventurers have dreamed up over the centuries.

The most striking thing about the park would have been its centrepiece, the six bright blue glass domes of Oceana. These six interlocking bubbles would have been balanced on a podium of diagonally thrusting rockwork, unlike anything the Imagineers had ever produced before. But in keeping with other Disney parks, DisneySea would also have had its own Princess' castle, and of course the underwater realm's resident Princess would have been Ariel, the Little Mermaid.

The largest sphere would have housed a huge water ride on a seven million gallon natural lagoon. Guests would travel in spherical capsules on a journey through the evolution of the seas and past the many extreme habitats below the surface of the ocean waves.

The ride would pass by an underwater volcano, dark, fearsome ocean trenches and even visit the freezing polar ice-caps.

Also in Oceana would have been the massive 'Oceanarium', a two storey series of aquariums featuring marine habitats and ecological systems from around the globe, and an Exploratorium of knowledge about the seas. Here would have been hands-on opportunities for guests to learn of the power of a tsunami for example, or to operate giant crab claws.

For smaller visitors there was Pirate Island, a children's adventure area where, with a little help from Disney's attendant buccaneers, they could follow clues which would lead them to buried treasure.

Guests would also have been able to observe and interact with real oceanographers and marine scientists working at the Future Research Centre. Just like Epcot's Living Seas, these scientists would be carrying out real research as well as answering guests' questions. If visitors found this area too educational for them, there would also have been a thrilling underwater exploration simulator ride named Nautilus 2000.

A full sized Egyptian galley ship would sit on the water as part of the Fleets of Fantasy area, as would a mysterious Chinese Junk. Other unusual boats would fill the water of DisneySea along with more rides as well as shops and dining.

Heroes Harbor would be the land where myths and legends of the sea came to life. At its entrance would be the Aqua-Labyrinth, a maze with walls that were constructed entirely from sheets of running water. The voyages of Ulysses and Sinbad would form the back stories of two rides in this part of the park, and overlooking everything would be the Mysterious Island, with Jules Verne's Nautilus submarine resting in dock at its base. This section of DisneySea would have been housed entirely inside a huge hollow volcano which would dominate one side of the park. The two headline rides here would have been The Lost City of Atlantis and Captain Nemo's Lava Cruiser. The Lava Cruiser was to be a roller coaster ride which would have suspended riders beneath the track in swaying ore carts and hurtled them through the dangerous caverns of the underwater volcano, eventually erupting in a blast of steam.

The Lost City of Atlantis (also known as Escape From Atlantis) was a more gentle boat ride. It would take riders on a winding route through the remains of a lost civilisation amid crystalline passages. But this voyage wasn't without its own perils, as the boat fought its way past threatening whirlpools, volcanic eruptions and even an encounter with a sea monster.

Do some of these ideas sound familiar? As we've seen before with other projects, this section of the park would borrow heavily from the abandoned Discovery Bay plans.

Steel cages would allow the more intrepid visitors to descend into real shark infested waters, while the less brave could wade through fish-filled pools. There would be a snorkelling area where guests could explore sunken ships for pirate treasure, or they could simply enjoy reproductions of some of the most beautiful beaches of the world beside Venture Reefs. These Greek, Asian and Caribbean themed areas would house DisneySea's main shopping and dining areas.

Traditionalists would be happy to note that this most untraditional of Disney parks would be served by a brand new monorail loop, with the monorail passing right through the largest of Oceana's bubbles. And just like the other Disney sites around the world, nightfall at DisneySea would bring a huge fireworks display.

But that only covers the theme park section of the proposed development. Outside the DisneySea gates would be the rest of Port Disney, an entire district of entertainment stretching along both sides of the Queensway Bay area of Long Beach. The World Port would feature the mix of shops, clubs, restaurants and cinemas we've come to know through the Downtown Disney developments, as well as five themed hotels for guests to stay in.

And true to its name, Port Disney would be an actual working port, a home berth for up to five of the twelve planned ships in the newly-proposed Disney Cruise Line. There would also be a new four hundred berth marina for private use as well as a large public park spreading over both sides of the bay.

Further along the waterfront a spectacular Boardwalk Fun Fair section would evoke memories of the post-war years. Its big draw would be an old-style coaster with exposed criss-crossed wooden beams. Much of the Boardwalk's carnival look would eventually be included into the design of Disney's California Adventure. For example early concept art for Port Disney clearly shows a Sun Wheel, exactly the same as the one eventually built at DCA.

Disney also owned two other attractions in the area; in fact they were a large part of the reason that the Long Beach site was first considered for development. They had recently taken over the running of the Queen Mary cruise ship, and she would sit proudly at the edge of Port Disney. This opulent floating hotel would make an excellent place for DisneySea guests to stay, with some versions of the design even giving the grand ship a haunted hotel makeover, complete with man-made ghosts in some of the rooms. Right next door to her was the company's second recent acquisition, Howard Hughes' massive aeroplane The Spruce Goose, housed in its beautiful dome.

Add to this the five new hotels that were planned for the area and you'll see that Port Disney would have been an incredible undertaking. The land simply wasn't there to build on, so Disney proposed that approximately two hundred and fifty acres of Los Angeles' San Pedro Bay be filled in to accommodate the development. Sadly, this alone made it highly unlikely to come to fruition in its original form.

The concept was eventually dropped as the company announced it would instead be investing in the Westcot expansion of Anaheim's original Disneyland.

As ever though, good ideas never die. Many of the Port Disney plans were eventually incorporated into the designs for Tokyo DisneySea in Japan. That park opened in September of 2001 and includes Mysterious Island alongside a Sinbad's Seven Voyages ride, both originally slated for Long Beach. There's also a transatlantic-style steamer called the S.S. Columbia that looks quite a lot like the Queen Mary.

So Port Disney was destined for the scrapheap. But at least the company was still going ahead with Westcot... wasn't it?

Death of the Dream

Let's recap. In the early 1990's Disney planned to undertake a massive expansion in California. Firstly, in 1990, came the announcement that the company was to build Port Disney and DisneySea. Then the following year they went public on plans for the Westcot park and expansion of Disneyland. But the company made it clear that, while they intended to eventually develop both sets of plans, there was only cash available to build one of them, at least initially.

Whichever site was chosen would be expected to ease Disney's financial burden by providing the improvements to roads, utilities and sewerage management that would be required if the company were to make such a big investment in their area. More police and fire-fighters would also be required too, to ensure the safety of guests. Disney CEO Michael Eisner spelled this out quite clearly when he suggested to the press that the first large development would go to whichever city "wants us more".

The city of Anaheim would have been expected to build all necessary parking facilities if Westcot went ahead. Conversely, if Long Beach were to win then it would have to foot the bill for at least some of the horrific projected landfill costs, because the major downside of Port Disney was that it would have required a big chunk of San Pedro Bay to be filled in. There was even talk of using land excavated from the Anaheim site to fill in the bay as part of the Long Island development.

Whether or not the company was deliberately playing the two local governments against each other we'll never know, but the mayors of Long Beach and Anaheim were both making the right noises. Long Beach's Ernie Kell attacked Anaheim's "horrendous traffic problem" and asked "If you had a day to spend out on the water - on the ocean or on an island – or inland in the smog, which would you choose?" At the other proposed location Fred Hunter, the Anaheim mayor put his side of the argument more succinctly, simply stating that "Long Beach is of no concern to me".

Disney tried its best to keep both parties interested. It opened a Port Disney visitor's centre, while at the same time it bought up an additional precious twenty-three acres in Anaheim. But the price of land was becoming a further complication at both sites.

Unlike in Florida, where Walt had his staff quietly buy much of the property that would eventually make up Walt Disney World before making any announcement to the public, both Westcot and Port Disney would require enormous land purchases to be made after the company's proposals were out in the open. If the landowners knew how desperate Disney were for their property then the likelihood was that they would hold out for higher prices.

Both sets of designs underwent literally hundreds of changes in an effort to keep everyone happy. The Westcot plans were amended after objections were raised about the effect that the increased number of visitors and employees would have on the area, and of the noise from concerts at the open-air Arena. Disney made the mistake of trying to ignore the protesters as insignificant and unrepresentative of the local residents, but was dismayed to find an organised picket line at Disneyland's entrance during the busy and lucrative Christmas 1993 period. Also, the magnificent golden globe of Spacestation Earth was completely scrapped after complaints that it would dominate the local skyline. In later reworkings of the plans the reflective sphere was replaced by a three-hundred foot tall obelisk, which would shine a laser straight up into the sky.

The Long Beach project experienced problems with the locals as well. Environmental groups complained that the landfill required would contravene the state Coastal Act, so a year after DisneySea was initially announced, a second set of plans were released in October 1991. These designs greatly reduced the amount of landfill that would be needed.

However, the writing was on the wall. In late 1991, Disney pulled the plug on the entire Port Disney idea and the company gave up its lease on the Queen Mary and The Spruce Goose in 1992, allowing Howard Hughes' great plane to be moved to Oregon. But even though Anaheim seemed to have beaten off the competition for Disney's park development money, that didn't mean that Westcot was actually going to be built.

In his autobiography "Work In Progress" Michael Eisner explained "Enthusiastic as we were about the concept of Westcot, the projected cost of building it simply grew too high." On July 17, 1995 Disneyland Resort President Paul Pressler proclaimed that the Westcot project was officially cancelled, and in 1996 its replacement, Disney's California Adventure, was announced.

So the dreams of Port Disney and Westcot died.

Didn't they?

Well, certainly in their original forms they did, but over the years various bits and pieces of these grand designs have come to life in other ways. For example in February 2001 Disneyland opened its second gate – Disney's California Adventure. It was located exactly where Westcot would have been, directly across a central plaza from the Disneyland main gate. This plaza also leads to a shopping and entertainment district which includes a new, spectacular hotel. Again, this echoes the original Westcot design.

The Paradise Pier section of Disney's California Adventure contains much of the Boardwalk idea that was originally planned for Port Disney. And of course the entire concept of DisneySea was resurrected for the expansion of Tokyo Disneyland. The Japanese park's Mysterious Island appears, from the outside at least, almost exactly as it was designed for Long Beach, as does the Sinbad's Seven Voyages ride. And the American Waterfront section of Tokyo DisneySea resembles a condensed version of Port Disney's planned waterfront.

Then there's Tokyo DisneySea's Hotel MiraCosta. Constructed like a small Italian pavilion, this beautiful resort allows guests for the first time to actually stay within the boundaries of a Disney theme park, just as the Westcot World Showcase designs had intended.

If you add to these the persistent but unsubstantiated rumours that the company is looking into the possibilities of building a Florida DisneySea park, it becomes apparent that Westcot and Port Disney have never really gone away; they've just been incorporated into other parks.

And as for Westcot's replacement?

Disney's California Adventure is a fine park. There's nothing wrong with it. It has some fun attractions and makes a great addition to the nearby original Disneyland.

But as we've said before, just imagine what might have been.

Chapter 12 – La Souris Arrive en Europe[*]

IT SEEMED INCONCEIVABLE THAT SUCH A TRIED and tested idea as a Disney theme park could fail to be as hugely successful in Europe as it already was in America and Japan. The largest percentage of non-American visitors to the U.S. parks were European, the company had constructed a beautiful park with some beautiful hotels to go with it next door to one of the world's most popular tourist cities. How could it possibly fail? They were so confident that it would thrive from day one that expansions were being planned even before the first visitors went through EuroDisney's gates.

Back in 1976, Disney's then-CEO Card Walker had begun making tentative plans for a European Disney

---

[*] The Mouse Arrives in Europe

park. After Tokyo had opened its own Japanese version of Disneyland in 1983 the speculation and planning began to get more serious, but then again by this time a Disney theme park was a hot property. Veteran Imagineer Jim Cora remembers, "We looked in our archives and realised that at one time or another nearly every country in the world had asked Disney to come and build a theme park".

Despite strong bids from two Mediterranean areas near the Spanish city of Barcelona, a location just half an hour's travel out of Paris was chosen over the 1,200 possible others as the selected site. They were the lucky city to receive the gift of almost guaranteed economic growth from Disney. What could possibly go wrong?

Unbelievably, the unthinkable happened. The French people just didn't turn up in the expected numbers. Neither did the rest of mainland Europe. And the British, who have traditionally made up a larger percentage of visitors to Walt Disney World than any single American State, did what they had always done; they continued going to Walt Disney World, which they perceived as a better – and cheaper - option. France's inclement weather (compared to California or Florida) didn't help, and neither did then-President François Mitterrand declaring that it was "not exactly my cup of tea".

Drastic measures were needed to ensure EuroDisney's survival, and all immediate expansions was put on hold. Sadly, the most significant savings could be made by shelving plans for an impressive new

Land which could have been the most ambitious single area to be built since the birth of Disney theme parks.

Discovery Mountain

When EuroDisney was being planned, one of its lead Imagineers was Tony Baxter. Baxter had been heavily involved in the aborted Discovery Bay project at California's Disneyland and, as so often happens, many of those old discarded plans were resurrected for this new venture.

While Discovery Bay was never going to be built in Europe as it had originally been planed for the States, adapting it and its theme representing the adventures of the great French author Jules Verne seemed to be an excellent idea for the Paris park. With just a few amendments the planned Parisian version of the Disneyland favourite, Space Mountain, could become the focal point of EuroDisney's Discoveryland. Renamed Discovery Mountain, it would have been a condensed European version of Discovery Bay. In fact by combining a trip to the moon, a mysterious volcanic island, and the voyages of Captain Nemo, Discovery Mountain effectively became a mini "Jules Verne Land" within the confines of Discoveryland.

The French Space Mountain – De la Terre à la Lune (From the Earth to the Moon) drew its inspiration from the Jules Verne adventure tale of the same name. It would have been positioned in the centre of a hollow volcanic mountain, with the Columbiad cannon which fires the moon-bound passenger trains being powered by the volcano itself. From the Earth to the Moon was eventually constructed much as originally envisaged, but this was originally going to be just one of many rides, attractions, and eating places housed within the walls of Discovery Mountain.

The huge volcano would have contained so much more than the magnificent Space Mountain ride. It was originally planned to be between two and three times the size of as the finished product, and would have been filled with other delights. As always, these ideas were not all considered at the same time – there simply wouldn't have been room to accommodate them – but all of the following concepts were suggested at one time or another.

The hollow centre of the mountain would have been home to a bubbling lagoon that would have been alive with geysers, fountains and waterfalls. The most remarkable thing about the lagoon however would have been the 200-foot long full sized replica of Captain Nemo's Nautilus submarine. The long-lost sub would have been permanently moored here in the hidden depths of the volcano.

Just as in the Discovery Bay blueprints, guests could have taken either a walk-through of the Nautilus (similar to the attraction that was eventually built just outside the Mountain at Disneyland Paris,) or relaxed with a meal at Nemo's Grand Salon, an amazing underwater restaurant. This high quality eating place would have had picture windows and portholes looking out of the walls and ceiling at the colourful fish and sea creatures as they swam among the ruins of the once-proud city of Atlantis. And naturally, this being where Nemo himself liked to eat, diners would have been entertained by pipe-organ music. Later plans named this restaurant Vulcania, and it was under this name that a similar eatery was built at Tokyo DisneySea's Mysterious Island.

However this gourmet restaurant would have been at the very highest end of the price scale. Less affluent Parisian guests, or those who hadn't booked a table far enough ahead of time for this most exclusive Disney dining room could have eaten at The Bistro at the Top of the World, a counter service dining hall situated in the very peak of the Mountain. An observation deck was planned for this area too, offering breathtaking views over the entire EuroDisney resort.

To reach these areas at the pinnacle of Discovery Mountain, the very rim of the hollow volcano, guests would have had the option of ascending in an ancient, rickety steel elevator. This lift would have only been for the bravest though, as it was to have been programmed to malfunction at its highest point and suddenly drop alarmingly into the pitch-black lift shaft. Riders would have plummeted down past steaming vents in the volcano wall, bouncing unevenly within the fractured lift shaft until mercifully and miraculously reaching solid ground again. Despite not being put into production at this point, this was obviously an early design for what would eventually become the Twilight Zone Tower of Terror.

The old Discovery Bay designs would also have been represented by a revision of the planned Hyperion Airship Flight. Small reproductions of the famous dirigible from Verne's Island at the Top of the World would have flown guests from the peak of Discovery Mountain over Fantasyland and into a station in Adventureland. This would have looked so much better and more atmospheric against the predominately grey skies of Paris rather than the clear blue of Florida or California.

Other possible attractions to be placed within Discovery Mountain were Discovery Bay's Magnetic Spiral ride, a simulator ride named Nemo's Lava Cruiser and, it almost goes without saying, a new railway station for the Disneyland Railroad trains to deposit guests at. Rather incongruously amid all these Victorian styled attractions, there were even plans to situate the ultra futuristic Star Tours within the Discovery Mountain boundary.

The outer shell of Discovery Mountain wouldn't have had its current verdigris tainted iron appearance either, but rather might have been a massive gleaming glass and metal structure. Other plans had it reverting to the original craggy mountain appearance of Discovery Bay's planned Mysterious Island.

If either of the less natural looks had been selected for the Mountain's walls though, park guests would not necessarily have had to enter from ground level. They would have had the option of travelling between Discovery Mountain and the Videopolis on one side, or The Timekeeper on the other via covered walkways high in the air. These were named La Voie Stellar - The Star Way. It's an indicator of how close these walkways came to being built that the places where they would have joined into the Mountain were constructed as planned and are still clearly visible as large portholes in the side of Space Mountain.

From this description of the original French plans, it can clearly be seen that there was much crossover and reuse in the designs of Discovery Bay, EuroDisney's Discovery Mountain, Port Disney's Mysterious Island and the section of Tokyo DisneySea that was eventually constructed under that name. This is possibly the best example of the Imagineers never completely discarding an idea, just saving it until the right opportunity for its implementation comes along.

Eventually the ambitious plans for Disneyland Paris' version of Tomorrowland were pared down to just the Space Mountain ride, but the Discovery Mountain concept was dropped so late in the day that the attraction signage and the ride cars had already been built with an ornate 'DM' logo included in their design. In fact the name change only occurred just a few days before the ride's inauguration, a modification that has been attributed to the marketing men wishing to link the ride with Disney's other world famous Space Mountains. It wasn't until the 2005 refurbishment that updated the ride to Space Mountain: Mission 2 that the 'DM' signs were finally removed from the cars of Disneyland Paris' signature attraction.

Discovery Mountain may never have been constructed as originally planned, but for those who know where to look the reminders were in plain sight for over a decade.

The Other Lost Attractions of Disneyland Paris

It wasn't just Tomorrowland that would have set the Parisian park apart from its American cousins. Original designs called for Main Street USA to be scheduled for a significant upgrade as well.

EuroDisneyland's Main Street was originally going to represent a later date than Disneyland and Walt Disney World's. The 1920's were a period of American history that Europeans would have been familiar with from their early movies. The birth of jazz, the speakeasy and James Cagney-style gangsters were to have been the French Main Street's focus. Imagineer Eddie Sotto explained, "It would be America represented by the visions of Chicago and New York cities as they have been embellished and idealised in Hollywood movies".

In keeping with this suggested time period, the horse drawn carriages that we're so used to seeing on Main Street would have been replaced by an electric elevated trolley which was to have run down one side of the street. Once again, this idea was later recycled. WDI brought it out again when they created Tokyo DisneySea, where it runs above the American Waterfront section of that park on its way to Port Discovery.

The Geyser Mountain ride that had been originally suggested for Disneyland's Frontierland was considered as a possible addition to the Paris park, under the name Old Unfaithful. This ride was to have lifted guests up on a column of water before depositing them back to safety but like so many others it was eventually shelved.

In spite of all these cancelled ideas, nobody was in any doubt that there was one thing that simply had to be built: EuroDisney had to have its own castle. The designers knew that with actual stone castles scattered around the European countryside, the fibreglass castles designed for the American parks would simply not be impressive enough. While the pink castle that was eventually constructed is certainly elegant and impressive, it's very different from the massive trio of bronze observation towers that were at one time suggested as a replacement for the more traditional castle. Once again, Jules Verne and H G Wells were the inspiration for this collection of viewing platforms linked by glass elevators and connecting tunnels high in the sky.

"Sleeping Beauty Castle at Disneyland was inspired by the Neuschwanstein Castle in southern Germany. This European influence was fine for building a castle in Anaheim, but the fact that castles exist just down the road from Disneyland Paris challenged us to think twice about our design." said Imagineer Tony Baxter. Fantasyland producer Tom Morris added, "For over a year we discussed what the castle at Disneyland Paris would become. Would it be a grandiose castle or a small charming one, a sand castle or simply a true to life one?". In the end they made an excellent fairytale choice. Le Chateau de la Belle au Bois Dormant that eventually took pride of place at the park's hub is, according to many visitors, the most beautiful Disney castle of them all. So EuroDisney got its castle, but some other plans, as ever, fell by the wayside.

One of the attractions developed furthest for this park before being discarded was a Beauty and the Beast audio-animatronic show. It would have been housed in a small building like the familiar Tiki Room show, with the guests seated around a central clearing. Audio-animatronic versions of the film's clock and candlestick characters Cogsworth and Lumiere were to introduce the show. A real life Belle would have continued the story in both spoken word and song and, at the opportune moment, she would have been joined by a huge audio-animatronic version of the Beast. A young volunteer from the audience would be brought forward to hand the creature a rose, which it would carefully take from the child's hand before transforming into the handsome prince at the attraction's climax.

As a companion to this show a dark ride based on the movie The Little Mermaid was also planned. In fact at least five different versions of a ride based on Ariel's undersea adventures have been designed over the years. The most developed of these would have seen guests travelling in huge seashells and would have included all the popular songs from the movie. The ride would climax with the guests being threatened by the huge tentacles of the sea witch, Ursula. Great effort was put into making the underwater section of the ride believable, so that guests would feel a real sense of wonder when the ride left the dry land and dived beneath the waves to visit the kingdom of Triton. This undersea ride is now rumoured to be lined up as part of an expansion for Hong Kong Disneyland.

While the diverse collection of architectural styles that make up Disney Village, the French version of Downtown Disney, is certainly interesting, it wasn't the favourite concept for the entertainment area. A New England style shopping and dining district was almost all of the design team's style of choice. Nearly every one of them picked this over the eventual eclectic mix. Only one person favoured the varied styles that were eventually settled on, but that person was Disney's chief executive, Michael Eisner.

While it's true that the park struggled initially, Disneyland Paris is on a somewhat better financial footing now, and there are plenty of plans for future development going ahead. One of the most interesting of these is the possibility of the Animators Palate restaurant coming ashore in France. This full-service restaurant is a big hit on the Disney Cruise Line ships. With the first course the décor, the waiters' clothes, even the food itself is black & white. Little by little touches of colour are added to the restaurant with each passing course. By the time the diners reach dessert, the entire place is a multi-layered riot of colour, as if it had been highlighted by an unseen paintbrush. It's a wonderful concept that could do well in a country where the presentation and consumption of food are seen as art forms in themselves.

The Walt Disney Studios became France's second Disney park when it finally opened in March 2002, but plans for this expansion were being drawn up even before EuroDisneyland's own opening ten years previously. Originally to be named the Disney-MGM Studios, the intention was to give the second park the same look and feel as its opposite number in Florida. The Imagineers planned to take the best of Walt Disney World's MGM Studios and improve on it. The Great Movie Ride was one of the attractions that would have been rebuilt in a bigger and hopefully better incarnation for the new French park, under the new name of the Great Movie Palace. A sound effects show was also to have been brought in, as were film sets based on New York and other streets around the world.

It had been hoped that Disney-MGM Studios Paris would open in 1994 as part of The Disney Decade but, like so many things announced under that banner, it wasn't to be. While it was a little later than planned in being open to the public, the new Studios has lost no time in generating its own expansion rumours. Toon Town could be a welcome major expansion in Europe, an indoor re-creation of the Roger Rabbit themed area that was initially suggested for Walt Disney World but is now at Anaheim's Disneyland. A version of The Tower of Terror, with or without its Twilight Zone overlay, is also supposedly on its way to the Walt Disney Studios Paris.

Another possible headline attraction has been planned based on the Pixar movie Cars. If it ever gets built, this will be an upgraded version of Epcot's Test Track ride. Whereas that ride places riders in the vital role of crash test dummies being subjected to extremes of heat, cold and speed, the Parisian Cars version of the ride might feature twin tracks, with the ride vehicles racing against each other.

One final attraction that has yet to be seen at Disneyland Paris is the Natural Kingdom - an entire expansion theme park populated by exotic animals as well as thrill rides. The Natural Kingdom was an idea for placing a smaller version of Disney's Animal Kingdom in the company's European park.

While Disneyland Paris is now attracting visitors from around the continent and beyond, it's fair to say that many French people were not in favour of the park being built in their back yard. And they weren't the only people to reject the idea of Disney building near to them.

Chapter 13 – The American Dream Expands

DISNEY'S AMERICA WOULD HAVE BEEN THE company's most patriotic theme park, and its design was a personal favourite of the man who helmed the Disney Corporation for some twenty years, Michael Eisner. Plans for Disney's America were unveiled in November 1993, showing the park that was to be situated on 2,400 acres of land at Prince William County near Haymarket, Virginia. The park would have brought distinct periods of American history to life, highlighting the conflicts and successes that have marked the country's two-hundred year passage from colony to major world power.

Eisner had visited Colonial Williamsburg, the restored 18th century town in Virginia, and wanted Disney's Imagineers to produce something similar to that, but with a liberal sprinkling of Disney magic. The Disney boss claimed that the park was to be solely themed on America because the country "is the best of all possible places, [the] place that you are happy you are living in. And if you're not living there, you would love to be part of the American experience". Above all, the concept was to represent the best of America as it had been in the past, how it was now and its hopes and aspirations for the future.

But even though it was designed to include up to nine themed lands, Disney's America was to be built on a much smaller scale to either of the established American Disney parks. The company thought that the public might see a day at Disney's America as complimentary to a trip to Washington (located just twenty miles away) and the historical sites that abound in that area.

A 19th Century "Main Street" area would form the entrance to the park. This street was to depict a much earlier date than the ones in the Magic Kingdoms, but would be no less detailed. The idea was to give visitors who had been to any of the other Disney parks around the world a sense of continuity as they started their day here before they diverged into the other less recognisable areas of the park.

A Native American village would accurately depict life as it had once been for the indigenous local tribes of the area. A white water river raft ride recreating the expedition of Lewis & Clark would wind around this wilderness section of Disney's America. This resurrected the widely respected Western River Expedition plans that had been intended for Walt Disney World's Magic Kingdom in the mid-1970's. This latest version of it would have been called Manifest Destiny, after the 19th century beliefs which lead to the Lewis & Clark expedition, that white Americans had a God-given duty to explore and tame the entire North American continent.

Elsewhere there would be a nightly recreation of the famous sea battle between the Merrimack and the Monitor. These two American Civil War warships fought the first ever sea battle between ironclad vessels, and would do so again daily on Disney's America's lake, Freedom Bay. Adjacent to the lake would be a large field, which would become the site of regular re-enactments of American Civil War battles. And as all Disney parks need a central icon, a pentagonal Civil War fort would be at this new park's hub, overlooking the lake and acting as Disney's America's surrogate castle.

A State Fair area would show how Americans are able to find entertainment even during times when they couldn't afford any, like the 1930's depression. A major highlight here was a live show based on that favourite American past-time, baseball, but it would also include older theme park fare that current visitors' parents or grandparents might remember, like an old-fashioned Ferris wheel and a wooden roller coaster.

A scale replica of the Statue Of Liberty was planned as the centrepiece for a section of the park representing the cultural diversity of the country. Alongside this small scale beacon of freedom would be a representation of Ellis Island, where visitors could experience a little of what so many American immigrants had gone through in this, their new country's entry point. This would be housed in a section of the park called We, The People, and would include selections of the food and music that the immigrant population brought with them to their new home. The civil rights movement, the Vietnam War and its influence on America, musical diversity - all these would be represented here too in We, The People.

In another part of the park the struggles of the country's immigrant population would have been told using Jim Henson's Kermit the Frog, Miss Piggy, and other famous Muppet characters. Although the idea might seem a little crass now, the company claimed that they wanted to interest young people in their country's history while also injecting a little humour into a subject that could all too easily have been made depressing and inaccessible.

The popular Hall of Presidents exhibit would also be installed here at Disney's America, although in a re-written format from the one that has been performing at Walt Disney World. The bad news for Floridians is that their Hall of Presidents show would probably have been removed and relocated to Virginia. The audio-animatronic attraction would have been the centrepiece of President's Square, the Civil War town region of Disney's America. This new version of the show would highlight the writing of the constitution and the birth of American democracy.

Victory Field would have celebrated the U.S. Air Force's contribution to the two World Wars. As well as simulators allowing guests to feel what it was like to fly a jet plane or sail through the air on a parachute, there would be hangars containing a major military museum. Alongside these attractions the designs called for the creation of an actual working airfield which, it was hoped, could be used for aerobatics displays.

One of the proposed park's major headliners would have been a roller coaster named The Industrial Revolution. This would have taken thrill-seekers through a true-to-life working steel mill, representing America's belief in success through hard work. The show building alongside the coaster would contain fully functioning blast furnaces and drop hammers, giving the rider a real sense of the heat and power required in forging metal.

At the smaller end of the scale would have been a display based on a family farm, where guests could try their hands at milking cattle and churning ice cream. And of course it should come as no surprise to hear that visitors would have been able to ride a circuit of the park's perimeter on an authentic steam train.

Lastly, and perhaps most controversially, Disney's America was to have included an attraction based on an attempt to escape from slavery. The Underground Railroad is a term given to the route by which African slaves took to freedom. Sometimes it was highly planned, sometimes spontaneous, but it was always dangerous. Had it been built, this attraction would have been wide open to criticism of insensitivity and trivialisation, but Disney's stated intent for this new venture was to create something that was "entertaining in the sense that it would leave you with something that you could mull over". A laudable idea, but it was probably a mistake to have an Imagineer in the press saying, "We want to make you feel what it was like to be a slave or what it was like to escape through the Underground Railroad".

To some observers the planned Disney's America was a celebration of all that was great about the country. To others, it was the worst excess of a heartless big business cashing in on a nation's identity. Even worse, it was to be located close to a Civil War battlefield at Manassas, a site of immense historical importance. There was much concern that the battlefield site, in the midst of an area of natural beauty, would be damaged or even completely destroyed by the huge development. So much concern in fact, that it became seen as a national battle between Disney and several conservationist groups.

As well as the location issues, Disney ran into problems with the proposed name for the park. To many people 'Disney's America' implied corporate ownership. It was fine for the company to have their own Land, even their own World was OK, but America is The Land of the Free, and its name belongs to its people. In his autobiography even Michael Eisner admitted that this was a contributing factor to the idea's eventual downfall.

One of the Imagineers that worked on Disney's America explained. "The intent of the project was to try and bring the informality of a Renaissance Faire together with the design sensibilities of a theme park. Unfortunately it is a lot easier to give a Renaissance Faire lots more money, while a theme park design 'machine' like WDI has a harder time thinking cheap. While a Renaissance Faire deals with dusty dirt roads and hay bale seats, theme parks work in cast concrete and air-conditioning, all budget busters". He continued, "The motivation for the park was really Eisner's desire to get closer to Washington and the powers that reside there. This of course was what finally killed the project as locals became outraged at the gall of 'Disney's' America somehow being 'better' than actual American history."

There was a further reason why the park wasn't ever going to be a success. Another Imagineering source explains, "in the end the park was very heavy in what we ended up calling 'boy' projects, since the team was predominantly male, and focused too heavily on war inspired exhibits and attractions. I think we felt the project was doomed months before we even announced, and the bad press just made sure the park was completely dead by repeatedly beating on its corpse for years after it was announced".

To try to at least remove the problems with the name, the ownership angle was removed in a later revision of the park's design. Disney's American Celebration would have replaced the previously announced Lands, with their references to specific periods of American history, with pavilions representing

Work, Family, Service & Sacrifice, and other aspects that together make up the 'standard' American. It still wasn't change enough though. The national press had come out in force against Disney on this, and the park's future was sealed.

Some last minute revisions of the plans, rebadged again with the name Disney's Waterfront, were also drawn up, but this too was short-lived. However had it gone ahead, people would have found that Disney's Waterfront would have been quite different from the original Disney's America idea. The Waterfront concentrated on the daily lifestyle of an era, focussing on urban elements like dining and retail. History was part of the makeup of this new concept, but to nowhere near the same extent as in the extravagant plans for Disney's America. The Waterfront was all about the way that Americans led their lives, and no longer about the history that made them who they are.

Whatever name it went under, this celebration of America was doomed. To add to all its other problems its budget ballooned to $625 million and beyond. At its most bloated the design included an entire housing district as well as the now-expected range of shops, hotels, and entertainment.

On September 28th, 1994 Disney announced that, while they still believed that the park would be a success, they would be searching for a different location. So far, none has been forthcoming, but in 1995, when ideas were being pitched for a second park to create a multi-day resort at Anaheim, Disney's America again briefly resurfaced. The idea was rejected again though, in favour of a California-themed park. However it would seem that at least some lessons had been learned, as the park was named Disney's California Adventure, not simply Disney's California.

Texas Disneyland

While Disney's America had been a fully planned concept, a Texas Disneyland seems to be less so. The state of Texas has often been suggested as a possible home should the Disney's America idea ever resurface. While that looks unlikely, it should be noted that Disney purchased large areas of land in Texas' Orange County in the 1990's.

Some of this property, located not far from Houston, would possibly have been developed into a small park with a Western theme. There has even been talk of using some of the land as a Disney Cruise Line terminal. This would allow the ships to regularly sail on longer cruises from their home base of Port Canaveral in Florida through the Gulf of Mexico to Texas and beyond.

In the future Disney is planning on expanding further into cruising and other non-theme park related vacations. It is already operating escorted holidays in such places as the Yellowstone National Park and Hawaii under its Adventures By Disney banner. These vacations might be a lucrative expansion for the company as guests require greater vacationing choices while retaining the security of booking through a company they love and trust. Almost any vacation anywhere in the world then becomes possible, all operated by Disney.

But as yet even Disney hasn't developed its own ski resort.

Mineral King Ski Village

Walt Disney had always loved skiing, but by his mid-sixties his health troubles were worsening, making it an uncomfortable pastime for him. His legs stiffened up in the cold and the pain in his back and neck (from an old polo injury) was getting worse. He was also starting to have trouble breathing, as the lung cancer that would finally kill him was taking hold.

It was during the making of The Third Man On The Mountain in 1958 that his interest in the sport reached its peak. The film-makers were based at a resort in Switzerland and the ever-inquisitive Walt asked many questions about how the resort was run, how it had been planned, how they looked after their guests etc. He became convinced that this kind of operation could be done much better if it were his business. He had already invested in Lake Tahoe's Sugar Bowl Ski Resort, but was now starting to give serious consideration to owning and operating his own winter wonderland.

A couple of years later Disney was invited to stage various ceremonies for the Winter Olympics at Squaw Valley, California, and it was here that Walt met up with Bavarian ski expert Willy Schaeffer. Walt ordered surveys to be taken of various mountain sites in the U.S. and had Schaeffer check them out from the sporting angle. Aspen in Colorado, California's Mammoth Mountain and various sites in the San Bernardino range were all investigated, as was the beautiful Mineral King Valley on the edge of the Sequoia National Park in California. Eventually Walt decided on the undeveloped potential of Mineral King, and Schaeffer confirmed that the area would provide excellent skiing. In what has become their usual way of operating, the Disney Company began to quietly buy as much land in the area as it could.

Many people believed that the valley should have been included within the original scope of the Sequoia National Park, but the abandoned remains of a small and very short-lived town that had sprung up in the silver mining boom of the 1880's had been enough to exclude it. However, by the time of Disney's interest nature had reclaimed most of her own and the area was almost totally uninhabited.

In 1965, the United States Forestry Service began accepting bids from companies wishing to develop Mineral King valley. They had already invited potential developers in some twelve years previously, but had not received a single offer. This time they were looking for investments in excess of $3million. Five other bids matched this, but Walt showed how much potential he believed the site had by bidding a startling $35million. This was provisionally accepted and work began on planning the alpine resort.

Disney's Mineral King Ski Village would contain two hotels, ten restaurants, a chapel, a skating rink, a bowling alley, a theatre and of course various chair lifts to get the skiers to the slopes. As well as all this Imagineer Marc Davis designed an audio-animatronic show for the resort that would become part of Disney theme park history. The Country Bears were originally planned to be hibernating creatures that would have rather stayed warm indoors throughout the winter. As part of their deal to live alongside the humans they had to sing for their keep, hence their regular shows. This was a great, fun idea, and after the Mineral King project was cancelled it was deemed too good to be allowed to just fade away. It was installed in the regular theme parks and is still entertaining guests to this day.

For the ski resort, Walt had planned to only allow vehicles access to the mouth of the valley, taking people the final leg of the journey by train or monorail. It was important that the area not be polluted either atmospherically or visually by having lots of cars and busses around.

In September 1966, Walt and local Governor Edmund Brown held a press conference at the relatively inaccessible valley to announce plans for the resort and the highway that would service it. Walt said, "It is our plan to make Mineral King a year round recreational adventure for everyone. A challenge to the accomplished skier and a good place to put skis on for the first time. The ideal spot for an old-fashioned family outing. Home base for wildlife students, hikers, fishermen, and campers. The perfect retreat for those who just want to get away for a breath of fresh, invigorating mountain air".

These were encouraging words, showing that even in later life Walt was still thinking big. But something was wrong. Reporters commented on how frail Walt looked as much as they spoke about the mountain project, and they were right. It was to be his final major press conference. Walt Disney died just three months later.

Despite Walt's death, work continued on planning the ski resort. The size of the proposed development surprised many. While the original Forest Service plan had been for accommodation for around 100 people per night and day parking for approximately 1,200 cars, Disney's proposal was somewhat more ambitious. 3,000 guests would be accommodated overnight along with up to 3,600 cars. Future expansion plans suggest that Walt had ideas for 20,000 skiers to eventually enjoy the slopes. There would be eight ski lifts serving four ski bowls. To get all those people to the resort, the existing road system would have to be dramatically improved. Unfortunately some eight miles of the suggested new highway would be required to cut straight through the

Sequoia National Park. With access roads through U.S. National Parks generally being forbidden, this raised conservation problems. What had seemed to Walt to be a way of allowing thousands of people access to one of nature's most beautiful areas was now being questioned because of the effect that all those people would have had on the area and its wildlife. Was it morally correct or even legal to build such a large concern in the area?

Before long those same questions were being asked in court.

To make matters worse, in early 1969 a Disney employee was killed and several buildings destroyed as an avalanche swept through the valley. Naturally the question of ensuring safety at any resort to be built in the area was raised.

The legal process dragged on for over a decade, and the Disney Corporation was starting to lose interest as the cost of improving the road to the area spiralled while at the same time public support for the project was dwindling. The entire issue finally came to an end in October 1978 when the National Parks Acquisition and Expansion Bill was passed by Congress. As part of it Mineral King was added to the Sequoia National Park, removing any possibility of development in the area. Walt Disney's idea of a ski resort never came to fruition.

The Mineral King valley remains to this day an area of outstanding natural beauty, but very few people ever get the chance to see it.

Independence Lake

While the Mineral King plans were on their way to being abandoned, many of those same ideas were being put forwards again in the design of another outdoor recreation area in Northern California, Independence Lake. In July 1974 Disney announced plans to install the same kind of recreational development that had been planned for Mineral King at this site near Lake Tahoe in the Californian Sierra Nevada Mountains.

As with the earlier ski village plan, Independence Lake would be kept free from traffic and provide facilities for camping, summer and winter sports. This was in addition to walking & horseback riding in summer and skiing in winter. It was designed to be very much an all year round resort.

Unfortunately Disney could not acquire the necessary land from its owners, Southern Pacific Railroad and the U. S. Government. Once again, there was to be no ski village operating under the Disney name.

There may still be no Disney development in the Sierra Nevada Mountains, but the idea of a Disney Ski Resort has never really gone away. In the early part of the 21st century there was talk of the company opening a resort in Australia's beautiful Victoria state. Perhaps Walt's dream ski village might see the light of day yet.

Other Parks

Disney has never been in the business of restricting its best thinkers. The Imagineers have always had free range to develop fresh ideas and break away from conventional wisdom. Although the earliest Imagineers had never heard the phrases, these days we'd say that they were "thinking outside the box" or "pushing the envelope". They have over the years come up with ideas for brand new kinds of themed entertainment areas, completely different from the style of parks that we know.

Riverboat Square

St Louis, Missouri, was selected as the future home of Riverboat Square (also known as Riverfront Square), a small indoor theme park that Walt was considering in the early 1960's, with an announced opening date of 1967. The entire project would have been part of a huge urban renewal of the city's waterfront area, with Disney's Riverboat Square taking up an entire city block, mostly under a single roof to protect against the inclement weather.

As part of the attraction of Disneyland was its climate, the St Louis project would have featured a huge atrium at its heart, featuring trees up to five storeys tall, waterfalls and a river to give guests the feeling of being outdoors. If it had been built it would have been a very different kind of Disney park, one with a few rides but with greater emphasis on retail partnerships.

The Disney Backlot Tour

In 1987 Disney once again looked into the possibility of opening some of its Burbank property to the public with the development of the Disney Backlot Tour. However if things had gone to plan, this would not be like the other film studios' tours. In conjunction with James Rause' Enterprise Development Company they would have built an entertainment district including a number of nightclubs, restaurants and shows. They even went as far as publicly announcing that this forty acre entertainment marketplace would open to the public in the early 1990's.

The design was to include a tour of the Disney Animation complex alongside actual TV and radio studios. The only ride that was actually announced for the Backlot was The Great Movie Ride, a direct copy of the Florida theme park version, but there would be plenty of shows and clubs. Of course, being Disney, these clubs were going to be like no other, using technology from the theme parks to spice them up. Michael Eisner revealed that the effects used to create the Haunted Mansion ghosts would be used to create similar tricks in the nightclubs.

There would be ice and roller skating rinks, a ten-screen cinema, stages for live performances, and restaurants in this marketplace, but also over a third of the property's space would be dedicated to shopping.

One of the most amazing portions of this complex would have been an extremely high-class place for Disney fans to stay while they shopped and partied. Rooms and suites at the Hollywood Fantasy Hotel would all be individually themed around classic Hollywood movies. This would be the tallest and grandest building in the Backlot, featuring staff that were all going to wear replicas of famous movie costumes. Imagine seeing Marilyn Monroe at the check-in desk, Bogart's Sam Spade as a maitre d', or having your martini shaken – not stirred – by James Bond.

Topping off the hotel would be the Celestial Dining room, a restaurant on the topmost floor built inside a planetarium, so guests could watch the night sky change with the seasons while they ate - whatever time of night or day.

After the elaborate splendour of the hotel, the car park facility would have been pure folly. Its roof would have been the site of one of Disney's most highly themed swimming pools, to be named the Burbank Ocean. Plans had the theming (as well as a never-ending cascade of water) carrying over the side of the building and down the wall.

Later reworks of these Backlot Tour area plans show the same project as being called Downtown Disney, a name which was retained when the idea resurfaced near the theme parks at Florida and, later, Anaheim. California's version of Downtown Disney would, at its most ambitious, have linked the Burbank lot with the Anaheim theme park and resort via a large scale expansion of the monorail system. There was also talk of turning the Los Angeles Coliseum and its surrounding area into an ESPN sports entertainment district, much like the Disney's Wide World of Sports complex at Walt Disney World. This expansion would have also hopefully seen an NFL American Football team move back into the Coliseum. Disney even went as far as holding initial talks with the Carolina Panthers and the Seattle Seahawks in the hopes of enticing one of them to move their football franchise to L.A.

Sadly this was to be another planned development that the paying public would never see, but the land at Burbank that had been earmarked for the Disney Backlot was eventually developed by the company. It became the Disney Animation building and the company's multi-storey car park.

Although the Backlot Tour never went ahead, Disney was always keen to make their parks available to more people. But even Walt himself might have been surprised at the international expansion in recent decades of the company that he founded.

Chapter 14 – A Global Enterprise

THE HONG KONG DISNEYLAND THAT OPENED IN 2005 was not the first development that the Walt Disney Company had considered for this area. In the late 1990's plans were drawn up for a small but very familiar looking Disneyland in Hong Kong which would be designed along the Disney standard of a central hub with radiating spokes. It was hoped that this would provide a marketing foothold for the Chinese economy. And as it was to be such a small park the Imagineers were, for the first time ever, allowed to include any idea from any of their parks around the world. This meant that traditional Magic Kingdom rides like King Arthur's Carousel and Autopia could be considered, but alongside these might be such unexpected attractions as the Rock 'n' Roller Coaster or Grizzly Peak river raft ride. An outdoor dinosaur-themed coaster was also designed as the embryonic Hong Kong Disneyland's first all-new headline ride. To date this has yet to appear, but it wasn't the only attraction to be designed for the park on Lantau Island.

Two attractions that are really popular in the American and Japanese parks are the castle and the It's A Small World ride. When Hong Kong Disneyland was in its original planning stages there was an idea put forward to combine these two attractions, to have the Small World ride, complete with its infectious song, running within the castle walls.

Hong Kong Disneyland opened to the public on the 12th of September 2005. The success or otherwise of this venture will largely dictate the company's theme park expansion plans for the foreseeable future. There are certainly already plans afoot for a second, much bigger park in China, a Disneyland to be located in Shanghai. If all goes to plan, this could open as early as 2012. How the people of Hong Kong take to their own Disneyland will have a large bearing on where, if at all, Disney expands next. If this smaller park proves to be a success in Asia, then we can probably expect to see other compact (and relatively cheap) clones of the existing parks appearing around that part the globe. Another site in Japan has been considered, as have locations in Australia and South America. Singapore, South Korea, Turkey and India have also been mentioned as potential future Disneyland settings, and plans for a theme park at Puerto Rico with the tentative name of Disney's Caribbean Adventure have also been discussed.

The most radical suggestion that was presented to Disney management, and the one that on the face of it was least likely to be green-lighted, has to be that of a floating theme park. The idea was pretty simple: instead of spending millions of dollars developing and creating a new version of a Disney park in some far-flung corner of the world which may or may not be the hoped-for success, why not take a ready-built Disneyland and move it to that location for a while? The park would be assembled on a gigantic floating island capable of crossing entire oceans and docking at pre-arranged ports on a never-ending world tour. For all those people who would never otherwise get the chance to visit a Disney park, this would be a Disney park coming to visit them. It might sound ludicrous, but the fact that Disney has even given it some serious consideration shows that, as in Walt's day, they still have a willingness to listen to any idea, however fanciful.

While this bold but ridiculously expensive idea has been rejected at least three times by Disney's top brass, the company has of course taken to the high seas with its hugely successful Disney Cruise Line ships. The Disney Magic and the Disney Wonder are in regular service around the Caribbean and have even taken guests through the Panama Canal to Los Angeles and Mexico, but there are already hopes for a third ship in the fleet to be constructed. Once this is done then one plan is for one of the older ships to move to service the west coast full time while the new vessel replaces it on one of the east coast routes. The 2007 European cruises that the Disney Cruise Line are undertaking have added an extra option for future regular sailings, and the well-established Alaskan cruise route has also been investigated.

Tokyo Disneyland

The Japanese Disneyland is the park with the fewest original unbuilt designs, and for good reason. When the park was given the green light it was on the understanding that it be as close as possible to the original Californian park. They worked on the premise that many Japanese people were travelling to visit the California park, and if that's what the Japanese people wanted, then that's what they would get. Over the years however it has been slowly building its own identity. In the late 1990s it was rumoured to be getting a radical revamp to its Tomorrowland section, to be renamed Sci–Fi City. As well as redecorating the entire Land several rides would have received upgrades, for example the revamped Hyper Space Mountain.

Two new attractions created for Sci–Fi City would have been the Sci-Fi Zoo, a combined audio-animatronic walk through and theatre show, and Rockit Bikes. These high speed transports would have been motorcycle versions of Disneyland's futuristic looking but highly temperamental Rocket Rods.

Tokyo Disneyland's regulars weren't too unhappy at not getting this expansion though, as they received a completely new and very different park – the astounding Tokyo DisneySea – instead.

On The Beach

Disney's Vacation Club is an increasingly popular timeshare-style flexible vacation plan. It has beachfront properties at the beautiful Vero Beach resort at Florida, and at Hilton Head Island in South Carolina as well as at their theme parks. But these weren't Disney's first plans for playgrounds by the sea. Back in the late 1950's when Walt was considering an east coast version of Disneyland, a deal was brokered that would have seen Disneyworld built at Florida's Palm Beach. The plan was simple; combine the fun of Disneyland with the fun of the beach and ocean.

Twenty years later, another seaside area was on the cards. Disney's annual report spoke of "a natural ocean beach playground for families visiting Walt Disney World" at Melbourne Beach on Florida's east coast. The company bought over a mile of prime beach and planned to offer it as a secondary place to stay. After spending time at Walt Disney World, guests could then drive or be shuttled the eighty miles to the beach where they could start the second leg of their two-centre Disney vacation.

And whatever happened to the Disney Vacation Club's Newport Coast Villas? This project was announced in 1994 to be built on the Californian coastline near Laguna Beach. It would have combined resurrected designs for the Mediterranean and Venetian resorts that had originally been planned from Walt Disney World, and combined them into a large holiday resort just a half-hour's travel from Disneyland.

However Disney eventually sold off the land and while a hotel complex resembling the Newport Coast Villas has eventually been built, it wasn't done by Disney. It became a Marriott resort.

Water Parks

While these beachfront ideas may not have come to pass, Disney was right to gauge the popularity of playing in the water as part of a vacation. Many visitors to Florida find that the weather is much hotter than whatever part of the world they reside in. That is of course one of its major selling points and a prime reason for Walt Disney World being located where it is. Walt knew that when it's hot and sunny people want to cool down in the water. That's one reason that both Disneyland and Walt Disney World were built inland from the beach; Walt didn't want to share his guests with this free resource. Never one to miss a chance for profit though, Disney has created a series of highly themed water parks to keep guests entertained and of course to keep them on Disney property. Firstly there was the now-defunct River Country, a gentle water hole. Today we have Typhoon Lagoon and Blizzard Beach, both filled with water slides and pools of all descriptions.

Like all the other ideas shown within these pages, Typhoon Lagoon went through many concept changes before the idea of a boat stranded on a tropical paradise was settled upon. Some of the more interesting options considered were a water-logged logging camp, an overgrown lost temple rediscovered among the waterfalls and pools of a misty jungle and, most bizarrely of all, a massive beached and ruined cruise ship.

Typhoon Lagoon and Blizzard Beach are hugely successful at Orlando, but they aren't the only ideas that the company had for watery entertainment.

After the success of the first Pirates of the Caribbean movie, a new water park based upon this popular theme park ride and film was devised. This would have had guests swimming and floating amongst dilapidated pirate ships still housing the remains of their skeletal crew. If this hadn't worked, there was also talk of a Sports-themed Water Park.

The huge surf pool at Typhoon Lagoon isn't the first man made wave machine at Disney's Florida site powerful enough for surfers to ride their boards. The Seven Seas Lagoon at the Polynesian resort was planned to host surfing at this Hawaiian flavoured part of property. A huge wave machine was installed beneath the waters of the lagoon and did indeed provide waves large enough to surf during testing. However, due to the size of the waves, it was decided that it could not go into regular use, due to the erosion of the beautiful beach.

Moving away from Disney's Florida property, a combination water park and aquarium was considered during the brainstorming sessions that resulted in Disney's California Adventure, and Disneyland Paris has had plans for its own water park drawn up. Named Lava Lagoon, this area would be totally enclosed beneath a clear dome. The backstory was that even though Paris isn't the warmest spot on the planet, this particular section of it, conveniently situated near to Disneyland's hotels, would be sitting directly over a thermal spring. It would be this heat, apparently rising directly from the earth's core, which would warm the water in Lava Lagoon.

Chapter 15 - Beyond the Florida Four

When people think of Walt Disney World, the mental images they conjure up are usually all of the fun attractions at the Magic Kingdom, Epcot, the Disney Studios and Disney's Animal Kingdom. But there is a whole world of entertainment to be had outside of the big four parks while never leaving Disney property. And if the Imagineers had got their way, there would have been a whole lot more.

Mini Golf

Some of Walt Disney World's 99 holes of golf are, quite rightly, rated among the best in the world. The USPGA regularly come calling on Disney to host tour events. The money men at the House of Mouse pretty quickly realised however that not everyone has the ability or desire to play a full eighteen hole round of golf while on vacation, especially not in Florida's typical ninety degree heat. They noted that along nearby International Drive there have been some very successful miniature golf courses springing up. If the tourists can line other operators' pockets, then Disney is always looking for ways to bring those tourists (and their dollars) back on property.

The result was Fantasia Gardens mini golf, a short course themed around the cartoon classic Fantasia. With its dancing hippos and alligator, broomsticks and Sorcerer Mickey, it's a very popular way to pass some vacation time. So much so that a second course, Winter Summerland (featuring a vacationing Santa Claus), was soon built. But Fantasia Gardens was only one of at least four completely different themed courses that were designed. One that came close to making the final cut was themed around outlandish headlines from the National Enquirer newspaper.

Disney Island

Walt Disney World's Swan and Dolphin hotels, the Yacht and Beach Club resorts and the Boardwalk complex all look out onto a beautiful lake. Crescent Lake is popular for boating and fishing, but even this small body of water holds its own place in the history of lost Disney attractions. Located directly behind Epcot, Crescent Lake was to be home to a second Pleasure Island styled night spot, Disney Island.

Disney Island was planned to be opened here during the late 1980's and would have been a horseshoe shaped island with the open ends facing directly towards the Yacht and Beach Club. Three tiers of entertainment would have each had their own collection of clubs, shops and restaurants, with each higher level stepped back from the lower ones, creating a promenade in front of each storey.

Two of the more interesting clubs proposed for Disney Island were Sphinx and Zeppelin. Sphinx would have been similar to Pleasure Island's Adventurer's Club, but with a magician theming. The Adventurer's Club contains a series of rooms – the bar, the library etc – all providing unique miniature comedy shows. They are partly improvised and include small scale gags built into the actual furniture and décor of the club. Thematically it brings to mind the glory days of the British Empire. Sphinx was to have been similar to this but built around the idea of a gentlemen's club for the Egyptian branch of the Magic Circle.

Guests who visited the Zeppelin dance club would get the impression that they were actually inside the gondolier of a travelling hydrogen airship, and would be able to view the night lights of the city moving far below them through portholes in the club's walls.

Eventually it was decided to leave the lagoon without a central island, and make the night-time entertainment integral to the proposed waterside Boardwalk hotel complex. Today the Boardwalk spreads along Crescent Lake and is much more than a hotel. It revives the glory days of the beachfront boardwalk with its dance halls and sports bar, shops and street entertainers. In the end the Imagineers took many of the enticements intended for Disney Island and simply moved them onto the mainland.

But just because there was to be no man-made island in Crescent Lake, that didn't mean that this particular body of water was being completely removed from Disney's entertainment plans.

The Lloyd Webber Connection

When the Fantasmic! show opened in 1992 it became an instant success at Disneyland, where it still performs to thousands of happy visitors every night. A mixture of water, film, fireworks and laser effects, it presents an after dark spectacular featuring the much loved Disney songs and characters. Walt Disney World would obviously benefit from its own similar production, but didn't want to simply replicate the Californian show. Everyone knows that if you want to produce the best, you have to employ the best. With this in mind, Disney considered commissioning none other than Sir Andrew Lloyd Webber to compose a brand new short production to be performed at the Florida park.

Specifically, it was to be performed on floating stages on Crescent Lake, the lagoon between the Boardwalk, Epcot and the Yacht and Beach Club. Lloyd Webber's show was initially hoped to be a twenty minute version of the biblical Noah's Ark story.

Once this idea was no longer in favour, Sir Andrew turned his attention to EQ, another nightly show to be performed outdoors, but this time based around the theme of horses. Again, the music was written and again, the show fell by the wayside. There is currently nothing except boats to attract guests to the waters of Crescent Lake.

However Crescent Lake isn't the only body of water at Walt Disney World with a storied past and no immediate future.

Raz Island

In the heart of Bay Lake, not far from the Contemporary Resort, is a small natural island. Legend has it that it was the sight of these beautiful eleven acres that convinced Walt that this was the place to build his Disneyland East. Before Disney bought the property it was known as Raz Island and was home to a small farm. It was renamed Idle Bay Isle when Florida's first radio DJ purchased it in the late 1930s. Delmar Nicholson, who broadcast under the name of Radio Nick, lived and grew fruit on the island for over 20 years before selling it on. The new owners were a group of local business men who let the island grow wild and used it as a hunting ground. They had retained the Idle Bay Isle name, but most Disney fans know it as the name that the company gave it when they took ownership. Discovery Island became a remodelled tropical paradise which was home to various birds and animals.

Initially Disney had thought of naming this piece of land Blackbeard's Island and installing all kinds of Pirate theming on it. By the time the proposed name had changed to Treasure Island, this theming had grown to include a replica of the Benbow Inn, Benn Gunn's fort and a semi-submerged copy of the wrecked ship Hispaniola, all taken directly from the pages of Robert Louis Stevenson's famous novel. In truth, the only substantial pirate relic to be constructed was a wreck of a much smaller craft, Captain Flint's Walrus.

Eventually the pirate motif was abandoned and the island was renamed Discovery Island. As such, it became a conservation and education centre, featuring two hundred and fifty different kinds of plants and almost a hundred and fifty types of exotic tropical birds and animals at its height. For many years, this idyllic refuge from the hustle and excitement of the theme parks was a popular attraction at Walt Disney World. So much so, that the company gave serious consideration to building its most exclusive guestrooms actually on the island. There would have been just four Honeymoon Cottages among the foliage, each of the highest quality that Disney has ever planned.

Discovery Island closed in 1999, exactly twenty-five years after it opened. It was thought to be in direct competition with Disney's newly opened (and vastly more impressive) Animal Kingdom park. Since then it has remained off-limits to the public, but around the turn of the century there was a plan to reopen it as a live action version of one of the most popular computer games of all time, Myst.

Myst Island (also known as Mysterious Island) would have allowed a small number of paying guests to live out the events of the problem-solving game. They would be marooned on the island and spend the entire day working out various puzzles and conundrums. Exploration and ingenuity would have replaced the more conventional theme park thrills in this most unusual Disney attraction. Interestingly, the makers of the original Myst game claim that they took much of their inspiration from that favourite Disney Imagineering resource, Jules Verne's Mysterious Island.

Another possible use for the island was as a children's sleepover area. This would require the island to be renamed Camp Hakuna Matata, a supervised mini-summer camp complete with scheduled activities including nightly visits from the much-loved Lion King characters.

Any of these ideas might have brought this beautiful piece of land back into daily use but at the moment it stands idle, just a lovely little island that guests hardly notice as they sail past it on the way to the Magic Kingdom.

The Disney Mall

These days there is a Disney Store in most major cities, but at one time the Disney company gave consideration to creating its own entire shopping mall. DisneyQuest and the Disney Store would both be represented here, as would one of the short-lived Club Disney children's play areas. But many other retailers would have been invited to place an outlet at the Disney Mall. There were even plans to include a few small rides, but the mall's primary attractions would be retail and dining. One Imagineer described it as "a shopping / dining mall concept on steroids".

Downtown Disney

The Disney Mall may have died on the drawing board, but the idea of a large shopping / dining / entertainment area lives on in the Downtown Disneys of Anaheim and Orlando. The themed nightclubs ensure guests are entertained well into the early hours, but there was one club designed for the Florida site that would have stood out from the rest.

This most indulgent club at Pleasure Island was to have featured a very special guest star. Madison's Dive would have been built on and under a pier stretching out into Lake Buena Vista. The underwater section of the club would have featured a large picture window looking out into the waters of the lake. Just like the Adventurers Club, Madison's Dive would have been filled with quirky characters spinning almost unbelievable yarns to entertain guests. One of these would have told the story of how an old sea dog once had an unexpected but very pleasant meeting with a mermaid. At the appropriate moment Madison, the beautiful mermaid from Disney's hit movie Splash, would appear at the under sea window.

Disney Downtown

Not to be confused with the Downtown Disney entertainment complexes, the company also suggested creating Disney Downtown, a planned after-school entertainment and educational complex for children. Sports, arts and music programs were to be set up, as well as other programs aimed specifically at under-privileged kids. State of the art music areas would replace the more traditional theme park fare with the likes of flyover tunnel walkways that were actually musical instruments. These sounded different tones according to the way a child moved within the tunnel. There would also be a painting studio for kids who's interests lay in that direction, with four-storey tall walls that could be used to produce temporary gigantic images.

Part of the Disney Downtown idea was to get young people interested in The Arts, to allow them to express themselves while removing many of the boundaries that might be perceived to be in place at a regular art school. If other children were more sports orientated, then they would be catered for too. Indeed the entire concept sprung from an Imagineer's plan for an indoor ice rink that could be doubled up for figure skating, soccer, volleyball, tennis, and other sports.

Naturally Disney Downtown would also have had its own shopping and entertainment areas. This has always been a part of the Disney parks. But after people have had fun at the parks, shopped, gone to a night club or to the cinema, Disney obviously doesn't want them to take their hotel room business elsewhere. That's why it runs one of the world's largest hotel operations.

But, just like the theme parks, there are many Disney resorts that never made it off the drawing board.

Chapter 16 - The Disney Hotels That Never Were

THE WALT DISNEY COMPANY HAS BEAUTIFUL hotels located at every one of its theme parks. Almost all tastes and budgets are catered for. But by now it should come as no surprise to learn that there have been plans for many other resorts to be built in, around and completely off Disney property.

Disneyland and Walt Disney World

Let's get personal for a moment; I love the Disney resorts. It's my firm belief that if you've been to a Disney park but stayed off site, you've only experienced half of the magic. Sure they're expensive, but for your extra cash you get the full Disney experience for twenty-four hours a day.

But the hotels and resorts we have available to us at Disney properties around the world today don't quite paint the entire picture. A vacation in a Disney hotel might have been a whole different experience if some of the rejected plans had got the go-ahead.

For example we've already seen how the remarkable Hollywood Fantasy Hotel would have astounded guests had the Disney - MGM Backlot Tour ever gone ahead at Burbank. And long serving Imagineer John Hench once designed a wonderful looking Mickey Mouse hotel which he hoped would have been built at Disneyland in California. The entire structure would have been shaped like the classic 'Hidden Mickey' three-ring or ball icon, sloping down on both sides so that its shape could be seen from the front or back of the building. Sadly, it never got past the design stage, but there are many other equally impressive Disney resort plans over the years that have come quite close to actually being constructed.

Further down the Californian coastline at Long Beach, there would have been five new hotels if Port Disney / DisneySea had been developed as originally planned. Port Hotel was to have been a small, luxury hotel attached to the resort's World Port entertainment district, whereas the much larger Canal hotel would have housed 1,400 rooms and had its own marina for up to a hundred and fifty guests to moor their boats. On the city side of Port Disney would have been the nine hundred room Tidelands hotel, the Shoreline hotel which would have been made up of four hundred suites, and the seven hundred room Marina Hotel, located alongside the Long Beach Convention Centre. Sadly these never came to pass due to the cancellation of the entire Long Beach project.

One of the earliest set of plans for Walt Disney World suggested that an entire collection of Disney hotels should completely encircle the entire property, acting as a giant berm to keep the outside world at bay.

When the Florida property was in its later planning stages, it was going to include six resorts, including the Fort Wilderness Campground. This, the Polynesian and the Contemporary were all to have been in place from opening day. However the following three intended resorts were dropped.

Disney's Venetian Resort would have been situated on the monorail loop between the Contemporary and the Ticket and Transportation Center. This has been suggested as an expansion resort on more than one occasion and the company have even gotten as far as starting to clear the ground before pulling the project again. This Italian themed resort would have been the most luxurious resort accommodation that Disney has ever designed. Gondolas on canals would have transported guests from a central shopping, dining and lobby area to their rooms in small villas. Each block of guest rooms would have represented a different architectural style from around Italy. The area would have been dominated by a large campanile, an authentic replica of the famous tower in St. Mark's Square, Venice. Though the entire Venetian idea was eventually shelved, this bell tower was built almost exactly as originally conceived, and today stands at the entrance to the Italy Pavilion at Epcot.

Also on Walt Disney World's monorail loop was to have been the Asian Resort, situated where the Grand Floridian is now. This hotel came so close to being built that its huge foundation base reaching out into the lagoon was created and prepared for construction. The ground lay cleared but empty throughout the seventies, waiting for the green light but it was never given the go-ahead, so visitors never got to see this magnificent Thailand-themed property. It would have consisted of long blocks of guest quarters facing onto the water and surrounding a central courtyard with a swimming pool and the resort's restaurants, shops and administration centre in a single huge towered structure. The name of this resort would change frequently between Asia and Asian.

After the park opened, Disney's Persian Resort would have been the first expansion at Walt Disney World. This would have been located between the Contemporary and the Magic Kingdom, and would have looked much like the Sultan's Palace from the movie Aladdin with its white walls, cultured gardens, archways and magnificent golden onion domes. Its circular 'walled city' design would have made it unlike any other Disney resort. But, as we'll see again later, that patch of land was to remain undeveloped

Each of these first five hotels was designed to correspond with one of the five Lands of the Magic Kingdom. For example Tomorrowland would have been linked with the Contemporary

A later resort that was never built at Walt Disney World was the Greek island themed Mediterranean Resort, which would have been a relatively small deluxe hotel on the banks of the Seven Seas Lagoon near the Magic Kingdom. This expansion was planned for the mid 1990's but was sadly another design to be dropped. Models made at the time show how it would have featured simple, clean apartment blocks facing onto the water.

Obviously all these resort concepts had been designed to give Walt Disney World visitors a feel for different areas of the globe. However this was no longer required once Epcot had stopped being talked of as an actual functioning city and had changed to include the World Showcase. The hotels didn't need to represent foreign architecture; the much larger pavilions would do that now. But the idea of having Disney guests stay in various countries didn't disappear completely. It would be revisited in the designs for Westcot.

In more recent times Disney has expanded into the budget end of the room market with its All-Star resorts. But the All-Star Movies, Music and Sports resort blocks that we see today might once have been joined by All-Star Comedy and All-Star Theater resorts. There was also some talk of a Toontown Hotel to be built to the north of the Magic Kingdom, overlooking Mickey's Toontown Fair.

And at the other end of the budgetary scale there were to be the four exclusive and very romantic Honeymoon Cottages to be located out on Discovery Island. Can you imagine spending the first days of your married life with this beautiful secluded island wildlife sanctuary all to yourselves after it had closed for the night?

The site between the Contemporary and the Magic Kingdom that had been earmarked for the Persian Resort has often been talked of as a site for the Kingdom Suites hotel. This was to have been a luxury hotel complementing the Contemporary, but with all guests staying in their own superior multi-roomed suites, hence the name. This has been close to getting passed on more than one occasion, but the success of the vacation club apartments has seen Disney executives cool to the idea of building hotel suites. Maybe the Kingdom Suites themselves could be constructed as part of the Disney Vacation Club at some point?

If Disney had built all the resorts it planned to during the 1990's there would have been no less than twenty-six hotels on property in Florida. One of the most eagerly anticipated by those in the know was Buffalo Junction, a highly themed resort which was announced by the company but which has yet to materialise. Buffalo Junction was also known as Fort Wilderness Junction and would have provided a physical and thematic link between the Fort Wilderness

Campground and Fort Wilderness Lodge. The idea was to have a 'timeline of accommodation', allowing guests to walk from one to the other and 'travel through time'. The early American pioneering days of log cabins and camping would have been represented by Fort Wilderness Campground, and then Fort Wilderness Junction would have provided early western housing. Carrying on towards the present time, guests would pass the rustic self-contained cabins that had originally housed the men who (so the back-story goes) built Fort Wilderness Lodge. These are the Fort Wilderness Vacation Club apartments. Finally the present-day National Parks vacation hotels would be represented by the magnificent Fort Wilderness Lodge.

If Disney's Wilderness Lodge area had been developed to the fullest design, its construction could have included plans to link the entire woodland retreat together in a small Boardwalk style entertainment district. The guest favourite small steam train that used to run around the Campground for four years in its early days was to have been resurrected to pull its passenger carriages between all these areas. Actually the plans for Wilderness Lodge had been around since the early designs of the park in the 1970s, but it was going under a different name then. If it had been built twenty-five years earlier as intended, it would have been called the Cypress Point Hotel.

But what would Fort Wilderness (or Buffalo) Junction have looked like? It was to be a resort themed like a small "Wild West" town, complete with horses on sawdust streets. Guests were supposed to have the impression that they were staying on the set of their favourite Western movie. This resort was to the same basic design as the popular Hotel Cheyenne at Disneyland Paris, complete with a copy of Disneyland Paris' much-loved Buffalo Bill rodeo dinner show.

Other options that have been considered for Walt Disney World include the Eagle Pines resort, a golf-themed Disney Vacation Club resort to be built near the world class golf course, and an early version of a New Orleans mardi-gras themed hotel. Initial plans for the Port Orleans resort had it located at the side of the Disney Village shopping area, with the Empress Lilly riverboat docked at the resort's berth. This was to eventually become Walt Disney World's Downtown Disney shopping and entertainment complex.

Perhaps one of the most imaginative hotel ideas was letting guests actually stay inside the Disney Studios' Hollywood Tower Hotel, the building better known to thrill seekers as The Tower of Terror. This would have been an elaborate homage to a time when movie stars were like Hollywood royalty, and the hotels that they stayed in treated them as such. Unsuspecting guests would watch in horror as one of a seemingly normal bank of elevators would plummet at an alarming rate, depositing its screaming passengers right into the hotel's lobby. All the other shafts would contain normal elevators. Guests would just have to be careful about choosing which one they rode.

Beyond The American Parks

When the EuroDisneyland resort in Paris was in its planning stages, the initial designs had a collection of hotels grouped in an almost urban development, linked by a network grid of roads. In an effort to inject some Disney magic into the design, Michael Eisner invited top architects from around the world to submit hotel designs. These would be loosely themed around the concept of America or Americana. This theme was chosen because they felt it would make the resort stand out from the surrounding French architecture and also, as America is the favourite tourist destination for Europeans, Disney hoped the look would be well received by its new neighbours.

The invited designers were given just three weeks to prepare their entries, and some of them were unusual to say the very least. A completely underground hotel was suggested, so that the natural beauty of the area could be retained. It's difficult to imagine how that was linked in with the Americana theme, nor how the design of a completely clear hotel made entirely of Perspex and glass fitted in either.

More obvious, though just as unlikely to be accepted, was the idea of a hotel shaped like an aircraft carrier, which its Austrian designer Hans Hollein thought represented America and its perceived military strength. Not surprisingly, this idea wasn't considered suitable for a Disney Resort.

A Fantasia-themed hotel, complete with a giant iconic Sorcerer Mickey figure was much more likely to be approved. The design was at the lower end of the budget range, and was similar to that of Walt Disney World's All-Star and Pop Century resorts. One different concept with a rather confusingly similar name was The Hotel Fantasia. This was completely unrelated to the classic Disney movie, but would have been a grand Las Vegas-themed resort. Unfortunately in the end the company decided that they couldn't afford to fund both this and the magnificent Disneyland Hotel, so the Hotel Fantasia was dropped.

In its original plan the impressive Sequoia Lodge hotel would have been called the Forest of the Giants. Instead of the collection of mountain wilderness lodges that the resort holds today, its first incarnation had the buildings actually located in the branches of giant sequoia trees. Sadly the man-made 'trees' proved too costly and fraught with safety issues, but the name survived to the final product.

Some of the more fanciful ideas suggested for Disney's Paris hotels included a huge Goodyear blimp floating atop a tower, a cruise ship sailing on a sea of grass and an abstract, red circular hotel containing a small marina. Unsurprisingly, none of these made the final cut.

We are also still waiting to see the four Nature Villages that Disneyland Paris announced to the world in 2003. The Ranch, Sport, Water and Earth areas were to have been built near the Davy Crockett Ranch, some way away from the parks (unlike the majority of Disneyland Paris' accommodation, which is within easy walking distance of the main entrance). These four discrete mini-resorts would offer relaxation, access to nature, and sporting activates in a woodland environment, gently introducing the Disney experience to guests who may not necessarily be inclined to visit the parks.

And one final note about Disneyland Paris. There has been talk of two new resorts next to Paris' Walt Disney Studios - The Flamingo and the Palm Tree. These would apparently be moderate value, 'fun' hotels, but the huge number of guest rooms already available at the resort mean it could be some time before any additional hotels are required.

While the recently opened Hong Kong Disneyland is taking plenty of bookings for its Disneyland Hotel and Hollywood Hotel, a third resort is already being planned to be built between these two. And Tokyo Disneyland is hoping for its own version of Disneyland Paris' Disneyland Hotel, right at the entrance to the Japanese park.

Not all of Disney's discarded hotel ideas were for their theme parks though. There was the remarkable Hollywood Fantasy Hotel that was planned for the Burbank development. And during his first week at the company in 1984, Michael Eisner investigated the possibilities of building a Mickey Mouse shaped hotel at the Disney Studios in California. This wasn't to be a dusting off of John Hench's classic three-ring 'Hidden Mickey' design that had at one time been planned for Disneyland, but instead would have been a hotel shaped like the traditional full Mickey Mouse figure, the kind you might see on a watch. He would have stood forty-five storeys tall, with one leg majestically on either side of Buena Vista Street. While this was a fantastic idea, Michael Eisner admitted, "In my heart I knew that a hotel shaped like Mickey probably was going too far. Still, by pushing the envelope and suggesting the impossible a lively debate was sparked". Later he recalled, "It made no economic sense, it made no creative sense, but it was a lark. I did know that there was more than form and function involved. I knew that architecture could create a business market that kids in Kansas City were going to tell their parents they wanted to go stay in a hotel shaped like Mickey Mouse".

Of course Disney hasn't only planned for guests to stay at their properties; there have been some plans for actual residential communities, and not just the town of Celebration which was developed near Walt Disney World. As we've already seen, Walt's original thoughts for Epcot were of an actual working City (or Community) Of Tomorrow, but the company also drew up little-known plans for Walt Disney World to feature a town of its own back in the mid 1970's. Lake Buena Vista Village would have been a small town with full-time residents, complete with its own downtown shopping and entertainment area. This retail section eventually became what we now know as Downtown Disney. Some of the residential properties were built but the idea of selling them as homes had long since fallen through. A proposition was put forwards to make them retirement homes for the elderly but this too was abandoned, and the buildings eventually opened to the public as the Vacation Villas, Fairway Villas, Club Lake Villas and Treehouse Villas – collectively the Walt Disney World Village Resort. Sixty of the Treehouse units were built, beautiful octagonal houses raised up on stilts and almost hidden amongst the trees, but the apartment buildings and condominiums were no longer in the company's plans. This collection of buildings would later become the guest housing for the Disney Institute, a residential learning centre that was situated where the Disney Vacation Club's Saratoga Springs resort has now been developed.

One of Disney's most ambitious hotel projects was suggested in the mid-nineties. The company intended to build a forty-seven storey Disney Hotel / Vacation Club property in New York's Times Square, complete with pixie dust lights twinkling around the outside of the building. Michael Eisner still regrets not following through with this idea, but he and the rest of the board saw it as an incredibly risky venture at the time, as Times Square and its surrounding streets was a very seedy area. Eventually it was decided that the gamble was too large, and Disney pulled out. In hindsight of course, it would have been a wonderful idea – visitors could see a Disney show on Broadway and then carry on the overall experience by staying in the Disney Hotel. Ex-Disney chairman Eisner apparently regarded the failure to move this project along as the most important business decision that the company got wrong during his leadership.

Westcot Hotels

If the expansion of Disneyland had gone ahead as planned in the 1990's, the construction of Westcot would have included six new hotels with a combined total of four thousand new rooms at the Anaheim resort. Disney Imagineers produced an ambitious design to build a second theme park on the land that was at that time the Disneyland parking lot. Of course this eventually became Disney's California Adventure but the original concept was to have included much, much more.

Westcot would have been the first Disney Park to have hotel rooms built into the actual attractions.

Like its Floridian counterpart, Westcot was to have featured a World Showcase style section dedicated to showing architecture from around the globe. Unlike the Epcot version however, this Showcase wasn't to have featured individual countries but rather 'The Four Corners of the World'. So there would be a European corner, an Asian one, an area representing Africa and a fourth corner to show the Americas, all arranged around a central lake. Each of these 'corners' would have included rides, attractions, shops, etc based around the global area they were representing. These would be presented in a series of six storey buildings. The big new twist would be that while the bottom three floors of the Asian, African and European pavilions held the attractions, on the upper levels there would be a limited number of exclusive guestrooms. These luxury living quarters would naturally be themed to represent the geographical region in question.

Imagineer Tony Baxter described this idea – which Disney referred to as the 'Live the Dream' program – thus: "When we started Westcot we said to ourselves 'Could we find a way where they are not just looking at the France Pavilion or the Japanese Pavilion but actually saying 'That's where I want to stay', and having that be your headquarters for your whole visit to Disneyland' ".

So which architectural styles would these rooms have replicated? Well how about staying in Renaissance Italy, London, Paris or Germany? Or a white marble palace based on India's famous Taj Mahal? Rooms styled after ancient Egypt and classical Roman and Greek were also planned, as well as a replica of the magnificent domes of St Basil's cathedral in Moscow. Canada, Japan, China – all these countries' representative buildings would have had rooms above them too, and all built to a very high level of comfort. But of course these guestrooms wouldn't be cheap;

prices were expected to be around $300 to $400 a night, and don't forget that we're talking about the mid 1990's.

The World Showcase 'Living The Dream' rooms weren't the only hotels that were planned for Westcot though. You may have noticed that I made no mention of the Americas pavilion featuring hotel rooms. That's because there would have been three brand new hotels built outside the park's boundaries with more of an American feel, these in addition to the Disneyland hotel which was already in existence.

The new hotels would have been the Disneyland Resort Hotel, The Magic Kingdom Hotel and the Westcot Lake Resort. These new resorts would have been located on West Street, which would have been renamed Disneyland Drive as part of the development. Even though this was well before the Disney's California Adventure park was dreamed up, these resorts were to have architecturally resembled famous Californian buildings.

For instance The Magic Kingdom Hotel would have had more than a passing resemblance to the historic Santa Barbara Mission, while the Westcot Lake Resort was to have been built in the style of the Beverly Hills Hotel. This 1,800-room hotel would have been built in a horseshoe design curving, as its name suggests, around a six-acre lake. However these two moderate price range retreats would have been upstaged by the vacation area's flagship hotel, the 800 room Disneyland Resort Hotel. This luxurious complex was to be constructed in the style of San Diego's world famous Hotel Del Coronado, which would later prove to be such an inspiration for the Grand Floridian at Walt Disney World.

And on top of all that there was to be a new tower added to the original Disneyland Hotel. For the guest who wanted to stay at the Disneyland Resort, there would be plenty of accommodation choice.

Epilogue

SO THERE YOU HAVE IT, A COLLECTION OF abandoned concepts by Disney's greatest thinkers from Walt Disney himself through to the company's current crop of Imagineers. Is this a complete list? No, not even close. For every plan represented here there will have been many, many more ideas that have never made it outside of a Disney planning session or an artist's studio.

Walt Disney himself knew that all good plans have to go through several stages of reworking to turn them into great plans. As he said, "Get a good idea and stay with it. Dog it and work at it until it's done, and done right." Or as one Imagineer put it, "The reality of theme park design is that any project can come up with dozens of possible attractions within its life cycle. I am sure we came up with five hundred different possible attractions that never made it past the brainstorming stage. Some we sketched up, but all in all what was presented was what we felt was the best we could do for the money, and the most fun experience we could deliver."

Another current Imagineer put it more bluntly: "There are designers who have worked at WDI who in ten years have never seen one of their designs built."

It should be noted when reading all the tantalising descriptions printed here that each of these plans will have been changed many times from their original conception to their eventual cancellation. What I've collected within these pages are representative descriptions of each of the attractions mentioned. Had any of them got as far as construction then they would certainly have been amended many times more before actually opening to the public.

And just because an entry has been made under one park's heading, that doesn't mean that it wasn't considered for other Disney parks around the world. There are plenty of rides and attractions that will have been rejected for one location, only to resurface at another. Then there are all those plans that the Imagineers haven't been able to fit into any of the parks - so far. Imagineering has an archive - known internally as 'The Morgue' - that houses miles of drawers filled with concept art for attractions that were proposed but never built. Disney never completely rejects an idea, even the really old ones. Chief Imagineer Marty Sklar explains, "Walt's original ideas are still very much alive.

We never really forgot about them, it was just a question of saving them for the right moment".

Within these pages there are descriptions of many entire theme parks, individual attractions, rides and hotels take from the pens, brushes and keyboards of the Imagineers. What you won't find in most cases however are reasons for these new developments' non-appearance. Sometimes the reasons were financial, sometimes political. Others were simply the victims of poor timing. The reasons are usually many and varied. But that's not what this book is about: it's about simply informing you, the reader, of what might have been.

It is also extremely important to note that Imagineering is a team process. Nothing goes from concept to construction in the hands of just one person. Many talented people work on an attraction, and they are usually among the best in their field at what they do. Remember, while Disney haven't yet been able to find a place for the planned marvels described in these pages, they have given us the most beautiful theme parks in the world and filled them with some of the most amazing rides and attractions ever seen. Consider Orlando's Twilight Zone Tower of Terror, Paris' Space Mountain, Tokyo's Mysterious Island, or Great Moments with Mr Lincoln. Only the skilled craftsmen and women at Disney could have produced these wonderful attractions, as well as providing their guests with the opportunity to stay in some world class hotels. Disney has raised expectations of quality far above those of its competitors. It has become a global brand name to whose success all others aspire. In his later years even Walt conceded "I'm not Walt Disney anymore". He spread his arms to indicate his beloved Disneyland. "All of *this* is Walt Disney."

One thing's for sure. While ever people keep flocking to their theme parks, then the Walt Disney Company will keep producing breathtaking rides and shows to entertain us for years to come. And who knows, perhaps some of the projects described in this book will one day be built at a Disney theme park somewhere.

Maybe even somewhere near you.

As the man who started it all once said,

"Disneyland will never be completed. It will continue to grow as long as there is imagination left in the world"

- Walter Elias Disney (1901 – 1966)

Acknowledgements

THIS BOOK WOULD NOT HAVE BEEN POSSIBLE without the help of the following people:

Paul and Ian, who got to say "I'd love to have seen them build that" before anyone else did

Gavin, for giving early drafts of some chapters an initial test run on his website, the wonderful www.mickeynews.com

Jill & Kathryn, my research assistants

My sincere thanks also go to the many present and former Imagineers who provided so much information and encouragement. The book you're holding would simply not exist without their considerable and extremely generous input. Any errors in the interpretations of their designs and descriptions are of course entirely my own.

I especially want to thank my parents for teaching me the joys of reading and writing, and for allowing me to dream the seemingly impossible dream that a boy from England might one day get to visit Disneyland.

And finally my thanks and love go to Jill for helping make that dream, and so many others, come true.

Bibliography

The Imagineers, "Walt Disney Imagineering", Disney Editions, 1996

Karal Ann Marling (ed.), "Designing Disney's Theme Parks", Flammarron, 1997

Dave Smith, "Disney A to Z: The Official Encyclopedia", Hyperion, 1996

Dave Smith, "Walt Disney: Famous Quotes", Disney's Kingdom Editions, 1994

Dave Smith / Steven Clark, "Disney The First 100 Years", Disney Editions, 2002

Kim Masters, "Keys to the Kingdom", William Morrow / Harper Collins, 2000

Michael Eisner, "Work In Progress", Random House, 1998

James B. Steward, "DisneyWar", Simon & Schuster, 2005

Leonard Mosley, "Disney's World", Stein & Day, 1985

Bob Thomas, "Building a Company", Hyperion, 1998

Bob Thomas, "Walt Disney An American Original", Hyperion, 1994

Andrew Ross, "The Celebration Chronicles", Ballantine, 1999

J. P. Telotte, "Disney TV", Wayne State University Press, 2004

Bill Cotter, "The Wonderful World of Disney Television", Hyperion, 1997

Marc Eliot, "Walt Disney Hollywood's Dark Prince", Andre Deutsch, 1995

Alain Littaye / Didier Ghez, "Disneyland Paris From Sketch to Reality", Nouveau Millénaire Editions, 2002

John Hench, "Designing Disney", Disney Editions, 2003

Eve Zibart, "Inside Disney", Wiley Publishing inc, 2002

Beth Dunlop, "Building a Dream", Abrams, 1996

Jason Surrell, "The Haunted Mansion: From the Magic Kingdom to the Movies", Disney Editions, 2003

David Koenig, "Mouse Tales", Bonaventura Press, 1994

David Koenig, "More Mouse Tales", Bonaventura Press, 2002

David Koenig, "Mouse Under Glass", Bonaventura Press, 1997

Monique Peterson, "The Little Big Book of Disney", Disney Editions, 2001

John Canemaker, "Walt Disney's Nine Old Men and the Art of Animation", Disney Editions, 2001

Jeff Kurtti, "The Art of Disneyland", Disney Editions, 2005

Jeff Kurtti, "Since The World Began", Hyperion, 1996

Jason Surrell, "Pirates of the Caribbean: From the Magic Kingdom to the Movies", Disney Editions, 2005

Richard Hollis / Brian Sibley, "The Disney Studio Story", Octopus Books, 1988

Robert Tieman, "The Disney Treasures", Carlton, 2003

Christopher Finch, "The Art of Walt Disney", Abrams, 1995

Bruce Gordon & Tim O'Day, "Disneyland - Then, Now, Forever", Disney Editions, 2005

936621

Printed in Great Britain by
Amazon.co.uk, Ltd.,
Marston Gate.